Contents

INTRODUCTION

Hello, everyone, and welcome to the Horrible Geography of the World. You're in for the trip of a lifetime, I don't mind telling you. And it's wicked to see so many of you here. I mean, you could be happily vegging out at home with your feet up and a bag of crisps. Instead, you've signed up for a trip into the unknown.

Before we set off, here's a word of warning. You might have heard the saying, 'It's a small world'. What a load of rubbish! The world's a very big place indeed and parts of it are horrible. Horribly cold and icy, or horribly hot and dry. On this trip, you'll be crossing raging rivers and scaling snow-capped freaky peaks. You might get hopelessly lost in the jungle or swept off your feet by a tornado. Wherever you end up, one thing's for sure. This tour's not for the weedy or faint-hearted. You'll need to be incredibly intrepid and hardy to make it back in one piece. Still keen to put your best foot forward? What's that? You've decided to stay at

home after all? Well, the rest of you better hop on board. It's time for us to hit the road.

Oh, I almost forgot. There's just time to introduce you to few of the other wicked world travellers who'll be joining us on this tour. Meet expert tour-guide and globetrotter Wanda, and her clever-clogs Uncle Cliff, who's a seriously brainy boffin. And last but not least, meet Parky, the penguin Wanda brought back from her last trip to the South Pole.

Now there's just one thing left to do before we hit the road, and that's to work out where exactly on Earth we are…

PLANET EARTH

To you, the Earth is home, sweet home – the centre of your universe. But to a slimy alien, it's an itsy bitsy blob of blue hanging about in the vast, inky blackness of space. Bet that's put you in your space, sorry, place. In fact, the Earth is one of eight planets (balls of rock or gas) that travel non-stop around the Sun. Technically speaking, our own particular bit of space is called the solar system. It's made up of the Sun, the planets, moons and other bits of space stuff.

FANCY A HOLIDAY THAT'S OUT OF THIS WORLD? WHY NOT TRY A BREAK ON ANOTHER PLANET? CONFUSED ABOUT WHICH HORRIBLE PLANET TO PICK? I PICKED UP THIS SERIOUSLY STRANGE SPACE GUIDE ON MY TRAVELS. IT'S COSMIC!

Horrible Holiday Guide: THE PLANETS

Mercury: For serious sun–worshippers, Mercury might be the planet for you. It's so horribly close to the Sun that daytime temperatures can reach a scorching 427°C!

Venus: Only recommended for the hardiest visitors. Venus's atmosphere is deadly poisonous and so horribly heavy it would squash you flat in seconds.

Earth: The perfect planet for you if you happen to be a human. Actually, it's the ONLY planet with the air and water you need to stay alive!

Mars: Nicknamed the 'Red Planet', it's famous for its pretty pink scenery. Trouble is, after you've seen a few hundred dusty, red rocks, you've seen them all.

Jupiter: There's loads to see on Jupiter – it's over 1,300 times the size of the Earth. Unfortunately, there's no solid surface to stand on – only a great big ball of gas.

Saturn: Saturn is another old gas bag, but it's well worth a visit for a view of its shimmering rings. Each one's made up of millions of bits of sparkly ice and rock.

Uranus: You'll easily spot this peculiar planet because of its ghastly, greenish tinge. This comes from mouldy methane gas in its awful atmosphere.

Neptune: One of the newest planets in our brochure, Neptune wasn't discovered until 1846. But with winds roaring at 2,000 km/h, the weather's likely to be woeful.

OUT OF THIS WORLD!

All systems go

So where did the solar system come from? How on Earth did the Earth get here? It all happened so long ago that no one knows for sure. Even Wanda's seriously brainy Uncle Cliff isn't that old. Here's what spaced-out scientists think might have happened:

1 About 4,600 million years ago, a colossal cloud of gas and dust starts spinning round.

2 Gravity (that's a force that pulls on things in space) causes the cloud to collapse.

3 The Sun forms from glowing gas in the centre of the collapsing cloud and begins to shine.

4 Specks of rock and ice in the cloud bump and clump together to make planets, including the Earth.

The sensational solar system

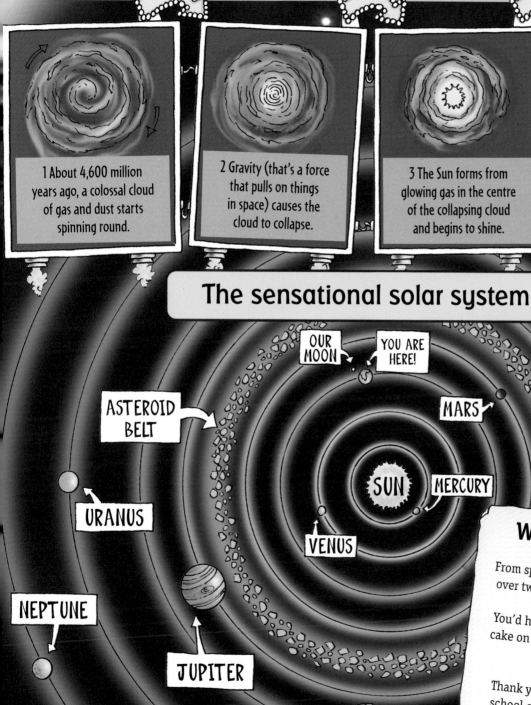

OUR MOON

YOU ARE HERE!

SATURN

ASTEROID BELT

MARS

URANUS

SUN

MERCURY

VENUS

NEPTUNE

JUPITER

7

WICKED WORLD FACTS

From space, the Earth looks blue because over two-thirds of it is covered by water.

•

You'd have a long wait for your birthday cake on Neptune. One Neptune year lasts for 164 Earth years.

•

Thank your lucky stars you don't go to school on Venus. One Venus schoolday lasts for 243 Earth days.

After your alarming space adventure, it's back down to Planet Earth with a bump. You might think the Earth is just a boring lump of solid rock, but scratch the surface and it's a whole different story. Underground, there are all sorts of warm and wobbly bits you can't normally see. Luckily, we've managed to get hold of an exciting X-ray to show you what the inside of the Earth really looks like. Here's Uncle Cliff with an in-depth look…

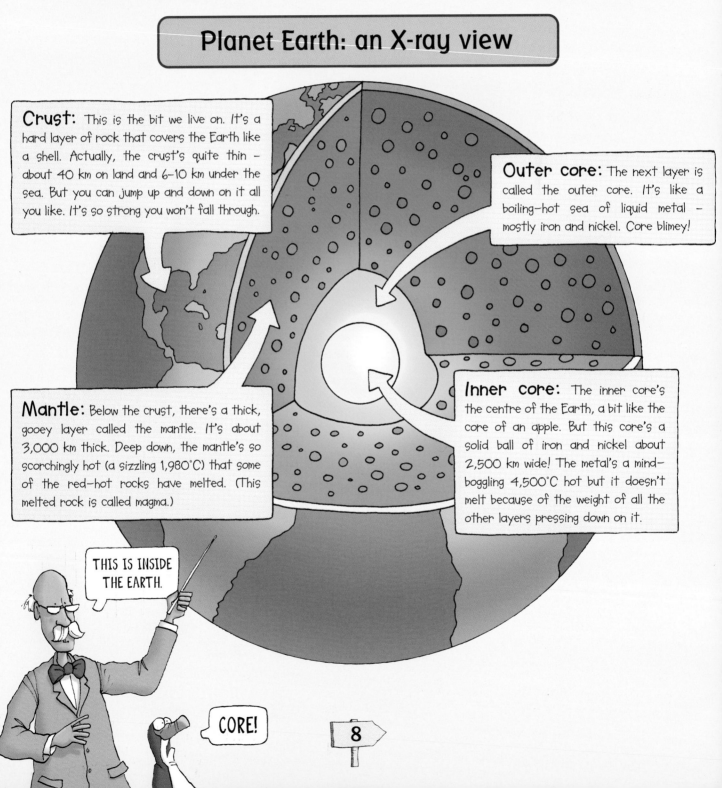

Planet Earth: an X-ray view

Crust: This is the bit we live on. It's a hard layer of rock that covers the Earth like a shell. Actually, the crust's quite thin – about 40 km on land and 6–10 km under the sea. But you can jump up and down on it all you like. It's so strong you won't fall through.

Outer core: The next layer is called the outer core. It's like a boiling-hot sea of liquid metal – mostly iron and nickel. Core blimey!

Mantle: Below the crust, there's a thick, gooey layer called the mantle. It's about 3,000 km thick. Deep down, the mantle's so scorchingly hot (a sizzling 1,980°C) that some of the red-hot rocks have melted. (This melted rock is called magma.)

Inner core: The inner core's the centre of the Earth, a bit like the core of an apple. But this core's a solid ball of iron and nickel about 2,500 km wide! The metal's a mind-boggling 4,500°C hot but it doesn't melt because of the weight of all the other layers pressing down on it.

THIS IS INSIDE THE EARTH.

CORE!

Crazy crust jigsaw

Picture the Earth as a gigantic boiled egg you've just bashed with a spoon. (OK, so you'll need to use your imagination for this bit.) The Earth's crust (the eggshell) is cracked into seven massive (and lots of smaller) pieces called plates. But forget the sort of plate you pile with yummy pizza. These plates are slabs of solid rock that float on top of the mantle. Is all this talk of food making you peckish? Or have you got enough on your plate? Here's Wanda and Parky with a handy map of the plates for you to feast your eyes on:

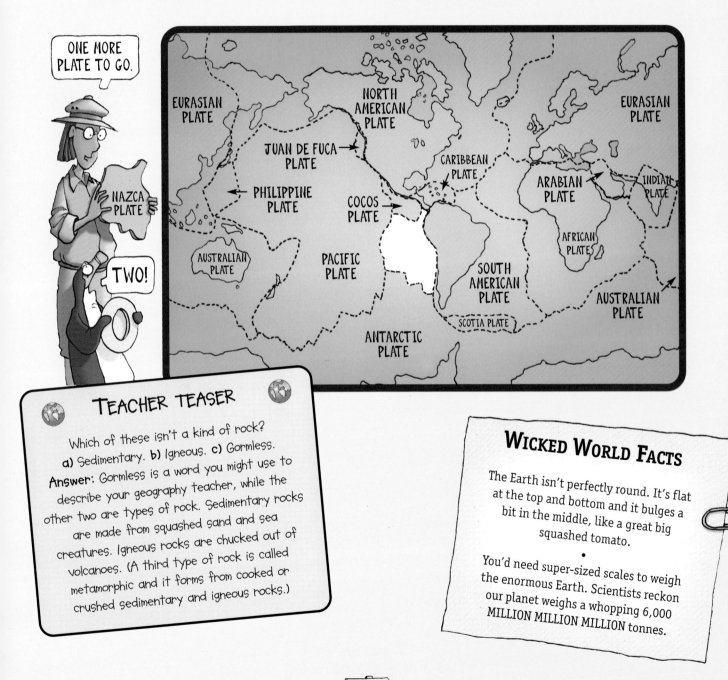

ONE MORE PLATE TO GO.

NAZCA PLATE

TWO!

EURASIAN PLATE

NORTH AMERICAN PLATE

JUAN DE FUCA PLATE

CARIBBEAN PLATE

EURASIAN PLATE

ARABIAN PLATE

INDIAN PLATE

PHILIPPINE PLATE

COCOS PLATE

AFRICAN PLATE

AUSTRALIAN PLATE

PACIFIC PLATE

SOUTH AMERICAN PLATE

AUSTRALIAN PLATE

SCOTIA PLATE

ANTARCTIC PLATE

TEACHER TEASER

Which of these isn't a kind of rock?
a) Sedimentary. b) Igneous. c) Gormless.
Answer: Gormless is a word you might use to describe your geography teacher, while the other two are types of rock. Sedimentary rocks are made from squashed sand and sea creatures. Igneous rocks are chucked out of volcanoes. (A third type of rock is called metamorphic and it forms from cooked or crushed sedimentary and igneous rocks.)

WICKED WORLD FACTS

The Earth isn't perfectly round. It's flat at the top and bottom and it bulges a bit in the middle, like a great big squashed tomato.

•

You'd need super-sized scales to weigh the enormous Earth. Scientists reckon our planet weighs a whopping 6,000 MILLION MILLION MILLION tonnes.

DRIFTING CONTINENTS

Remember the Earth's crazy-paving crust? Well, get this: the crusty plates might look rock solid, but they're constantly moving under your feet. They drift about on the layer of hot, gooey magma underneath. What's that? Don't worry. You won't get carried away. The plates usually move so slowly that you don't normally notice a thing.

A moving story

The person who worked out that plates move was German geographer Alfred Wegener (1880–1930). When eagle-eyed Alf looked at a map, he noticed that the east coast of South America fitted snugly into the west coast of Africa, like two pieces of a giant jigsaw. Alf reckoned they must have been joined together at one time and later drifted apart! Wicked. After that, the pieces just fell into place.

Here's Parky to show you how on earth we ended up with today's continents:

250 million years ago

All the continents are joined together in one colossal chunk of land, called Pangaea (that's ancient Greek for 'all lands'). Around it is an enormous ocean, called Panthalassa (that's Greek for 'all seas').

200 million years ago

Pangaea starts splitting in two. The bottom bit's called Gondwanaland. The top bit's called Laurasia.

135 million years ago

Gigantic Gondwanaland splits into Africa and South America, with the Atlantic Ocean in between. India breaks off and heads north to Asia.

40 million years ago

Australia and Antarctica start drifting apart. North America shifts west away from Europe, leaving Greenland as an isolated island.

PANGAEA

LAURASIA

GONDWANALAND

AFRICA

INDIA

SOUTH AMERICA

NORTH AMERICA

EUROPE AND ASIA

GET MY DRIFT?

Push and shove

Unfortunately for poor old Alf, no one believed a word of his crackpot theory. In fact, many geographers split their sides laughing. It wasn't until the 1960s that oceanographers* made a dazzling, deep-sea discovery that proved Alf was right all along. Here's how they might have reported their earth-shattering finds:

Important note 1

In some places, two plates of seabed are splitting apart and red-hot, runny magma spews up through the crack. And get this – when the magma hits the cold sea water, it cools and turns into hard rock ... making new bits of sea bed. So the sea floor is slowly spreading, pushing the continents further apart. Brilliant, isn't it? But why isn't the Earth getting bigger with all this extra rock? It's a mystery.

Note: must do more research into this.

Important note 2

Yippee! Yippee! We've got the answer. Oh, clever, clever us! Remember the spreading seabed? Well, in other places, we found the plates are bashing into each other instead of splitting apart. One gets pushed under the other and melts back into the Earth. This pushes the continents closer together. And guess what? The Earth stays the same size because, amazingly, the melting balances out the spreading. Exactly. Wicked, or what?

WICKED WORLD FACTS

Geographers call the way the plates move 'plate tectonics' (teck-ton-iks). Tectonics come from an ancient Greek word that means 'building'.

•

Coal is another crucial clue to the drifting continents. It's been found in icy Antarctica, proving that it was once warm and wet. That's because coal is made from trees that only grew in hot, tropical forests.

•

Alfred got his ingenious idea for the way the plates move while he was on holiday in Greenland. He was watching a load of icebergs drifting out to sea at the time.

Earth-shattering fact

Mesosaurus was an ancient reptile that lived about 300 million years ago. It looked a bit like a little crocodile and liked lounging around in swamps. What on Earth has a long-dead reptile got to do with drifting continents? Well, mesosaurus fossils are only found in Africa and South America – and nowhere else. Proving that these continents were once joined.

*OCEANOGRAPHERS IS THE POSH NAME FOR DEEP-SEA SCIENTISTS.

MUDDLESOME MAPS

Before we go any further, let's have a word about maps. There's nothing a horrible geographer likes more than gawping at a muddlesome map. See for yourself. Wave a map under your geography teacher's nose and watch her go all giggly and gooey-eyed. Pathetic. OK, so maps are seriously useful for looking at the wicked world and getting from A to B. (And tracking down buried treasure.) But are they really as boring as they seem or is there more to maps than meets the eye? Time to put maps on the, er, map.

Wicked world maps

Remember how the Earth is shaped like a gigantic ball squashed in a bit at both ends? Well, you can also get ball-shaped maps of the Earth called globes. But a globe's not very good for folding up and popping in your pocket. So geographers have worked out a cunning way of showing the Earth on a piece of paper. They unfold the Earth's surface and cut bits out of it to make it lie flat. The posh word for this type of map is a projection. Here's how to make your own projection out of orange peel:

You will need:

An orange, a knife and a good imagination.

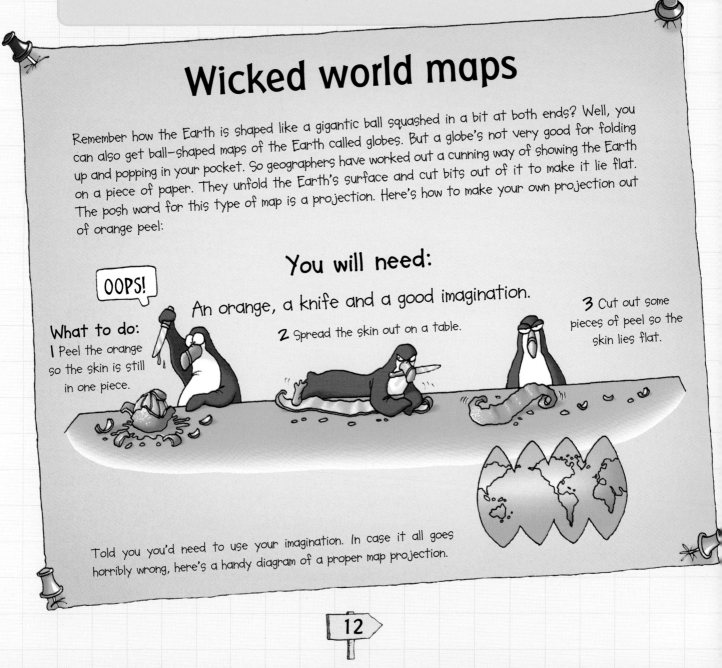

OOPS!

What to do:
1 Peel the orange so the skin is still in one piece.

2 Spread the skin out on a table.

3 Cut out some pieces of peel so the skin lies flat.

Told you you'd need to use your imagination. In case it all goes horribly wrong, here's a handy diagram of a proper map projection.

Lining things up

To help them plot where on Earth places are on a map, geographers draw loads of criss-crossing lines. They're called lines of longitude and latitude. But you won't be able to see them on the ground. They're not really there, you see. Anyway, by giving a place's longitude and latitude, you can pinpoint exactly where it is. Very clever, if you ask me.

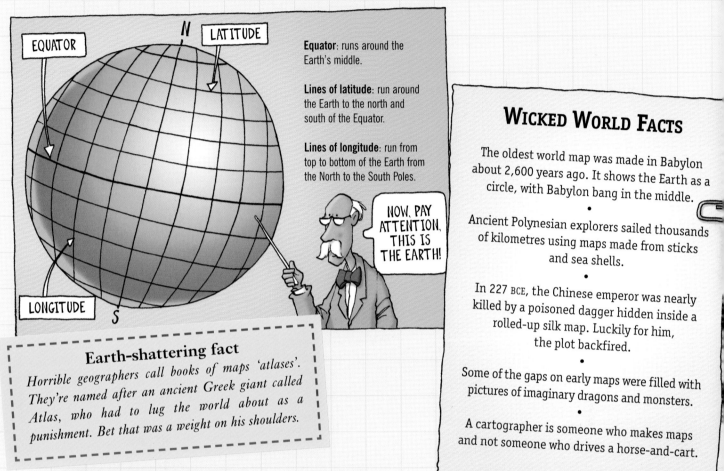

EQUATOR

N LATITUDE

Equator: runs around the Earth's middle.

Lines of latitude: run around the Earth to the north and south of the Equator.

Lines of longitude: run from top to bottom of the Earth from the North to the South Poles.

LONGITUDE

S

NOW, PAY ATTENTION, THIS IS THE EARTH!

Earth-shattering fact
Horrible geographers call books of maps 'atlases'. They're named after an ancient Greek giant called Atlas, who had to lug the world about as a punishment. Bet that was a weight on his shoulders.

WICKED WORLD FACTS

The oldest world map was made in Babylon about 2,600 years ago. It shows the Earth as a circle, with Babylon bang in the middle.

•

Ancient Polynesian explorers sailed thousands of kilometres using maps made from sticks and sea shells.

•

In 227 BCE, the Chinese emperor was nearly killed by a poisoned dagger hidden inside a rolled-up silk map. Luckily for him, the plot backfired.

•

Some of the gaps on early maps were filled with pictures of imaginary dragons and monsters.

•

A cartographer is someone who makes maps and not someone who drives a horse-and-cart.

Map-making

Early maps were simply squiggles on pieces of paper, stone or silk but today, muddlesome map-making has gone horribly high-tech. Here's how a modern Earth map is made:

1 A plane or space satellite flies over the Earth, taking masses of snaps.

2 The snaps overlap to build up a brilliantly detailed picture.

3 Once all this info is in, it's fed into a computer and it plots it all on an awesomely accurate map.

SHOCKING EARTHQUAKES

Picture the scene. One minute, you're strolling down the street, wondering what to have for tea. The next, the ground's shaking violently. It's an earth-shattering earthquake and it's got you quaking in your boots. But what on Earth is an earthquake? Find out in our seismic spotter's guide.

Seismic spotter's guide

Shocking earthquakes happen because the Earth's crusty plates simply can't keep still. They push and shove each other, putting the rocks under terrible strain. Soon the stressed-out rocks reach breaking point, and they jerk apart with a gigantic jolt, triggering an earthquake. The shakiest places on Earth lie along deep cracks where two pushy plates meet. These wobbly weak spots are called faults. But just whose fault is it? We sent Uncle Cliff to find out…

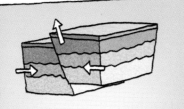

A) NORMAL FAULT
What to look out for: Two plates pulling apart so the rocks get horribly stretched.
Shocking sign: One plate sliding down under the other.

B) REVERSE FAULT
What to look out for: Two plates being pushed together, squashing the rocks in between.
Shocking sign: One plate sliding up over the other.

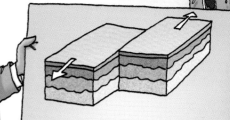

C) STRIKE–SLIP FAULT
What to look out for: Two plates sliding past each other.
Shocking sign: One plate slips one way; the other slips the other way.

WICKED WORLD FACTS

Seismic is the technical term for anything to do with earthquakes. It's ancient Greek for 'shaky'. Earthquake scientists are called seismologists (size-mol-lo-gists).

•

Most earthquakes last for less than a minute, but not the killer quake that hit Alaska in 1964. The Earth shook for four minutes – a lifetime in earthquake terms.

The quake that struck Lisbon, Portugal, in 1755 was so powerful that it sent water in lakes in Britain sloshing to and fro in whopping waves.

•

The 1,050-km-long San Andreas Fault streaks across California, USA. This is why cities like San Francisco, which sit on the crack, suffer thousands of tremors every year.

Earthquake X-ray

How does an earthquake happen? What sets off a shock? Here's Uncle Cliff again with an X-ray view of what happens when an earthquake strikes.

Fault: A giant crack in the Earth's surface. Most quakes happen here.

Shock waves: Giant, wobbly waves of energy that blast out through the rocks. When they hit the surface, they really shake things up.

Earth's crust: The rocky surface of the Earth, which is cracked into plates.

Epicentre: The place on the Earth's surface that lies directly above the focus. This is the shakiest spot in a quake.

aFocus: The spot deep underground on the fault line where the rocks suddenly snap. It's where earth-shattering shock waves begin.

Ten shocking earthquakes

Each year, a shocking one million earthquakes shake the Earth. Luckily, most of them are too weak to be felt, but about ten a year turn out to be deadly. Here's a map of ten of the most colossal quakes of the twentieth century.

1. 1964 ALASKA, USA (8.3–8.6)
2. 1906 SAN FRANCISCO, USA (8.3)
3. 1989 LOMA PRIETA, CALIFORNIA, USA (7.1)
4. 1985 MEXICO CITY (8.1)
5. 1970 CHIMBOTE, PERU (7.7)
6. 1960 VALDIVIA, CHILE (8.7)
7. 1988 SPITAK, ARMENIA (6.9)
8. 1976 TANGSHAN, CHINA (8.3)
9. 1995 KOBE, JAPAN (7.2)
10. 1923 KANTO, JAPAN (8.3)

Earth-shattering fact

Seismologists use the Richter Scale to measure earthquakes. It grades quakes from 1 to 8, depending on how much energy is blasted out when the rocks break (this is called magnitude). Each step up the scale means a tenfold increase in energy. So a massive magnitude 8 quake is actually ten times as powerful as a magnitude 7. Awesome.

Earth-shattering earthquakes are horribly hard to predict, so seismologists are under serious stress. If they could tell when a quake was coming, they could warn people and save thousands of lives. But how on Earth can they work out when and where an earthquake will strike next? It's a bit like being a doctor with one GIGANTIC patient. Over to you, Uncle Cliff…

PATIENT: Planet Earth

SINISTER SYMPTOMS:
- Masses of mini earthquakes
- Bright lights in the sky
- Rocks give off ghastly gases
- Geysers start gushing
- Water levels rise in wells

DIAGNOSIS: All of these warning signs seem to suggest an earthquake's about to strike. Then again, it might not…

TREATMENT: Mmm, this is the tricky bit. You can't stop a quake from happening, so my advice is … get outta there, fast!

SIDE EFFECTS: Earthquakes can be nasty. Very nasty indeed. Side effects include smashed-up cities, ripped-up roads, lethal landslides, fatal fires and sloshing tsunamis (soo-nar-mees – they're killer waves).

TRUST ME, I'M A DOCTOR.

HORRIBLE HEALTH WARNING

Of course, real earthquake doctors don't examine the Earth with a stethoscope. They use a posh bit of kit called a seismograph (size-mow-graff). It picks up the pattern of shock waves from an earthquake and traces it on to paper.

WICKED WORLD FACTS

The first practical seismograph was invented in the 1880s by the British scientist John Milne. Daring John's research included being tormented by tremors in Japan.

•

If you're indoors and an earthquake strikes, crouch under a table. Cover your face and eyes with your arms. Then hold on tight until the shaking stops (and you stop quaking in your boots).

If your pet dog suddenly stops chewing your dad's slippers and scarpers, you could be in for a nasty shock. Some people think animals act strangely before an earthquake. Your missing mutt might be trying to tell you a quake's about to strike.

•

In the 1985 Mexico City quake, two babies were pulled alive from the ruins of a hospital – ten days after it collapsed!

The good news is, seismologists can give very general warnings about where a quake might strike. The bad news is, they only know a quake's on the way when it's actually happening. To make matters worse, some quakes strike without any warning at all. Like the one that hit Tangshan, China, in 1976. Here's how the Daily Globe might have reported from the scene of the disaster.

DAILY 🌐 GLOBE

TANGSHAN, CHINA, 29 July 1976

The surviving residents of this shattered city are still reeling from the shock after yesterday's devastating earthquake.

Measuring a massive 8.3 on the Richter Scale, shell-shocked experts are already claiming the quake was the deadliest of modern times.

At 3.43 am, local time, a huge tremor struck without warning. In seconds, it reduced this thriving industrial city to a pile of rubble. Numbers are still coming in, but it is estimated that more than 300,000 people have died. Thousands more lie injured or buried beneath the collapsed buildings. Rescue teams have already begun a frantic search for survivors. Thousands of people have been left homeless. With winter coming, their future looks very bleak indeed.

MONSTER MOUNTAINS

Does climbing the stairs make you dizzy? Or do you have a good head for heights? You'll need to be in peak condition for the next bit of our tour. Yep, you've guessed it. We're heading for the hills. Only these horrible hills are at least 1,000 metres high, and are counted as monster mountains. Ready for some wicked views from the top?

Freaky peak fact file

For years, geographers hadn't the foggiest how monster mountains formed. Then brainy Alfred Wegener (remember him?) came up with his ground-breaking idea about how the continents drift. Yep, it's the way the crusty plates move that pushes up the different types of peaks.

Still wondering which mountain to climb? Why not check out our freaky peak fact file before you set off?

BLOCK MOUNTAIN

THERE'S A FOURTH TYPE OF FREAKY PEAK BUT YOU'LL HAVE TO TURN TO PAGE 22 TO SEE THIS BEAUTY BLOW ITS TOP.

FOLD MOUNTAIN

GLACIER

FOLD MOUNTAIN

Formation: Two colossal plates of crust smash into each other. The sea floor between them is squashed and squeezed into gigantic folds.

High points: Himalayas (Asia); Rockies (USA); Alps (Europe)

BLOCK MOUNTAIN

Formation: Forms at faults where two plates meet. As the plates push together, they shove up a huge block of rock in between.

High points: Massif Central (France); East African Mountains; Sierra Nevada (USA)

DOME MOUNTAIN

Formation: Magma deep underground seeps to the surface. It shoves the Earth's crust up into a nice, round hump.

High points: Lake District (England); Black Hills (USA)

Ten monster mountains

About a fifth of the Earth is covered in monstrous mountains. But just in case there isn't a freaky peak near you, here's a map of ten of the world's highest mountains and some of the longest mountain ranges.

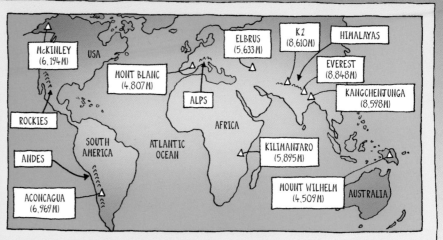

- McKINLEY (6,194M)
- USA
- MONT BLANC (4,807M)
- ELBRUS (5,633M)
- K2 (8,610M)
- HIMALAYAS
- EVEREST (8,848M)
- ALPS
- KANGCHENJUNGA (8,598M)
- ROCKIES
- AFRICA
- SOUTH AMERICA
- ATLANTIC OCEAN
- ANDES
- KILIMANJARO (5,895M)
- ACONCAGUA (6,969M)
- MOUNT WILHELM (4,509M)
- AUSTRALIA

A MOUNTAIN RANGE IS THE TECHNICAL TERM FOR A LONG CHAIN OF MOUNTAINS.

DOME MOUNTAIN

PEAK WEATHER REPORT
While you're admiring the view from the top, it pays to wrap up warm. The higher you go up a freaky peak, the colder it feels. The air's so thin and clear up there that it can't trap heat from the Sun. So even in the steamy tropics, peaks are capped with snow all year round.

TEACHER TEASER
Which is the highest mountain on Earth?
a) Mauna Kea. b) K2. c) Everest.
Answer: a) Mauna Kea's a vast volcano that pokes out of the sea in Hawaii. From its base on the seabed, it's a monstrous 10,203 metres high. That's more than 1,300 metres taller than earth-bound Everest.

Groovy glaciers

The slippery slopes of mountains are great places for glaciers. These are gigantic rivers of ice that slowly flow downhill. So how on Earth does a groovy glacier grow? Uncle Cliff's got the answer ... if he can stay upright. He's still a bit shaky on his skis.

1 Snow falls high up on the mountainside.

2 More snow falls and squashes it into ice.

PRETTY COOL!

3 Soon the ice is so heavy that it starts to slip. The steeper the slope, the faster it flows.

4 As the glacier flows, it drags along tonnes of rock, which grind out a U-shaped valley.

5 Eventually it reaches its snout. That's the end of the glacier, where it starts to melt. A bit like a runny nose. Aatchooo!

You need to be tough to live up a mountain. Never mind the bitter cold. What about the blinding blizzards and gale-force winds? Despite the hostile conditions, an amazing number of plants and animals make freaky peaks their homes. Time to meet some rock-hard mountain wildlife.

Horrible Holidays are proud to present their

MONSTER MOUNTAIN SAFARI

Fed up with boring beach holidays? Tired of lounging about in the sun?
Looking for the adventure of a lifetime?

WE HAVE THE ANSWER!

For a truly high-rise holiday, book now for our intrepid trip.

WILDLIFE WE HOPE TO SEE:

Klipspringers

This African antelope's so athletic, it can leap up and down sheer cliffs without losing its balance. Handy for escaping from enemies searching for a snack...

Yaks
High-rise yaks live over 6,000 metres up in the Himalayas, where it's easy to freeze to death. Luckily, their coats are so thick and woolly that they never even catch cold.

Springtails

These minuscule insects have black coats for soaking up the sun. Even so, they can live on mountains all over the world and spend most of their lives close to freezing point. Brrr.

Andean condors
Watch out for these high fliers in the Andes mountains. With wings as big as bed sheets, they soar above the slippery slopes on the look-out for lunch. Sometimes they scoff so much that they can't take off again.

Small print. Seeing any of these animals is not guaranteed. Sorry. After all, they've got better things to do than be gawped at by you lot. Like staying alive, for starters.

HORRIBLE HEALTH WARNING

Feel like you're being followed? Don't freak out. The chance it's a yeti is tiny. If you haven't heard of the yeti, it's a huge, hairy creature said to roam the Himalayan mountains. Is it a man? It is an ape? Nobody knows for sure, but similar creatures are believed to live in China, the USA, Australia, Russia and Africa. Trouble is, no one's actually caught a yeti yet – so they might not even exist at all.

It's official! Some hardy humans like to climb mountains … for fun! The higher, the better. Take daring British climber Edward Whymper. In 1865, he set off to climb the mighty Matterhorn in the Alps, even though people said it couldn't be done. If he'd kept a diary of that fateful day, it might have gone something like this…

Earth-shattering fact

Top Italian climber Reinhold Messner climbed all 14 of the world's highest peaks between 1970 and 1986. That's an awful lot of ups and downs.

MY MATTERHORN DIARY
by Edward Whymper

14 July 1865 1.40 p.m.
We've made it! We've actually made it. I'm writing this on top of the Matterhorn! And they said it couldn't be done. Pah! I set off yesterday morning with six companions, and we reached our camp by noon. Next day, we were on the move early. Luckily, the weather was brilliant and the climbing was easier than we'd thought. I was so excited, I ran the last bit.

Later that day…
Everything's gone wrong. Horribly wrong. On the way back down, disaster struck. We were all roped together for safety. Then, suddenly, one man lost his footing and slipped, dragging three others to their deaths. I still can't believe it. I only survived because the rope broke and stopped me plummeting…

HELLO!

WICKED WORLD FACTS

At 7,250 km, the awesome Andes in South America is the longest mountain range in the world.

•

Don't be surprised to find fossil seashells on top of Mount Everest. This freaky peak was once part of the ancient sea floor.

•

On some freaky peaks, tiny plants turn the snow pretty pink. The plants contain red colouring, which works a bit like sun cream. It stops them getting burnt in the seriously strong mountain sun.

All of the world's top ten highest mountains are found in the high-rise Himalayas.

•

Forget yaks and yetis. Ancient people thought mountains were so high and close to heaven that their peaks must be the high-rise homes of the gods.

•

If you start seeing things like yetis you might be suffering from mountain sickness. It's caused by the lack of oxygen high up. Get downhill … FAST!

VILE VOLCANOES

If you thought monster mountains were merely boring blocks of rock, you might want to think again. The freaky peaks you're about to watch are red-hot and bursting with energy. Yep, they're violent volcanoes, but how on Earth do they erupt? That's the burning question.

Exploding Earth

Most vile volcanoes erupt at the edges of the Earth's plates, where the crust is woefully weak and wobbly. Runny, red-hot magma from deep underground bursts or seeps up through cracks in the crust, building up a smouldering mountain. Here's what happens:

Volcano villains

As the lava cools and hardens, it builds up a mountain. But not all vile volcanoes are shaped like nice, neat cones. It all depends how thick the lava is and how violently they erupt. To help you pick which villainous volcanoes to avoid, we've lined up three smouldering suspects.

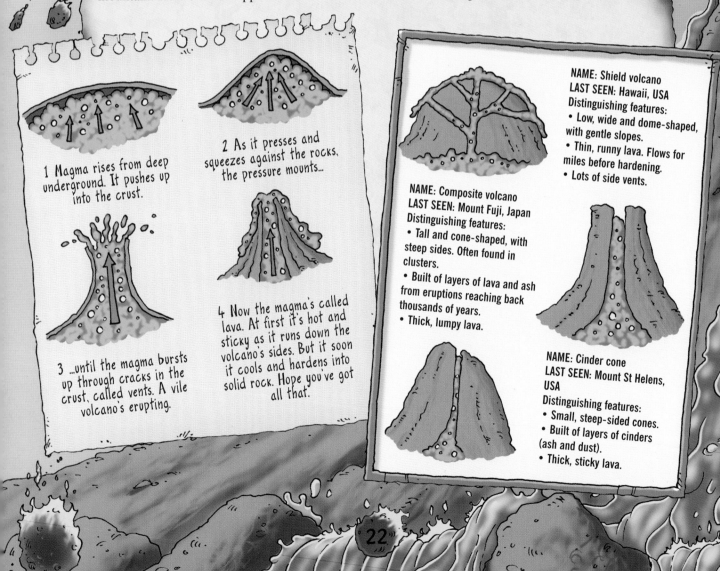

1 Magma rises from deep underground. It pushes up into the crust.

2 As it presses and squeezes against the rocks, the pressure mounts...

3 ...until the magma bursts up through cracks in the crust, called vents. A vile volcano's erupting.

4 Now the magma's called lava. At first it's hot and sticky as it runs down the volcano's sides. But it soon it cools and hardens into solid rock. Hope you've got all that.

NAME: Shield volcano
LAST SEEN: Hawaii, USA
Distinguishing features:
• Low, wide and dome-shaped, with gentle slopes.
• Thin, runny lava. Flows for miles before hardening.
• Lots of side vents.

NAME: Composite volcano
LAST SEEN: Mount Fuji, Japan
Distinguishing features:
• Tall and cone-shaped, with steep sides. Often found in clusters.
• Built of layers of lava and ash from eruptions reaching back thousands of years.
• Thick, lumpy lava.

NAME: Cinder cone
LAST SEEN: Mount St Helens, USA
Distinguishing features:
• Small, steep-sided cones.
• Built of layers of cinders (ash and dust).
• Thick, sticky lava.

WICKED WORLD FACTS

In 1883, Krakatoa erupted with a deafening bang. The noise could be heard in Australia, almost 5,000 km away.

•

The biggest volcano in the universe is Olympus Mons on Mars. It's three times higher than Mount Everest and has a crater the size of a city.

•

Volcanoes are named after Vulcan, the hot-tempered Roman god of fire.

•

Flaming liquid lava can flow at speeds of up to 100 km/h and reach temperatures of 1,200°C!

Ten awful eruptions

There are about 1,500 active (still erupting) volcanoes on Earth. Only about a third of them sizzle away on land. The rest lie underwater. About 50 of these vile volcanoes blow their tops every year. Here's a map of ten of the most awesome eruptions of all time.

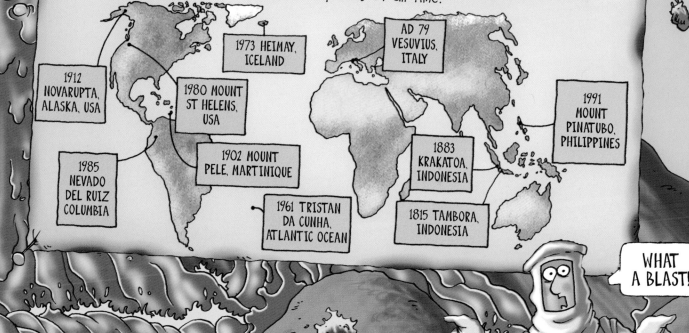

1973 HEIMAY, ICELAND

AD 79 VESUVIUS, ITALY

1912 NOVARUPTA, ALASKA, USA

1980 MOUNT ST HELENS, USA

1991 MOUNT PINATUBO, PHILIPPINES

1902 MOUNT PELE, MARTINIQUE

1883 KRAKATOA, INDONESIA

1985 NEVADO DEL RUIZ COLUMBIA

1961 TRISTAN DA CUNHA, ATLANTIC OCEAN

1815 TAMBORA, INDONESIA

WHAT A BLAST!

Living near a violent volcano can be horribly hazardous. It may snooze away for years on end, then suddenly wake up with a start. So what's it like when a vile volcano turns nasty? Hopefully, you'll never find out. The islanders of Heimaey in Iceland were not so lucky. On 23 January 1973, their world was turned upside down.

Here's how an eyewitness might have described the violent events…

HORROR IN HEIMAEY

It was the middle of the night, I remember. My friend and I were walking home from the harbour after our night-shift at the fish factory. Suddenly, we saw a wall of flames in front us. The ground was on fire! As we watched, a huge, gaping crack opened up and started to chuck out thick black ash and burning cinders. We ran for it and raised the alarm. The island was evacuated. Most people left for safety on the mainland. Meanwhile, the volcano carried on erupting. The crack grew wider and wider, splitting the island in two. Everywhere, houses were bursting into flames. But worse was to come. A lethal river of lava was heading towards the harbour. Now we were really worried. Without the harbour, we'd have no fishing industry … and no Heimaey.

A few of us stayed behind to try to save the harbour. We had to act fast. But how could we stop the lava before it blocked the harbour entrance? The situation seemed hopeless. Then someone had an idea. We drove all the island's fire engines down to the harbour and sprayed the lava with millions of litres of sea water. Incredibly, it worked! After weeks of hosing, we stopped the lethal lava in its tracks. Soon afterwards, the crack closed up and people were able to come back home. The eruption was over. For now, at least…"

PLANNING A NICE, QUIET HOLIDAY? WELL, STEER CLEAR OF PLACES AROUND THE EDGES OF THE PACIFIC OCEAN. IT'S NOT CALLED THE 'RING OF FIRE' FOR NOTHING. HERE THE SEA FLOOR IS BEING DRAGGED BENEATH THE LAND, TRIGGERING OFF VIOLENT VOLCANOES AND EARTHQUAKES. INDONESIA'S PARTICULARLY RISKY WITH ABOUT 125 PERILOUS PEAKS.

WICKED WORLD FACTS

The name 'geyser' comes from an old Icelandic word which means 'to rush up'. So now you speak Icelandic!

•

You'll get a crick in your neck watching Steamboat Geyser in the USA. It regularly gushes up to 115 metres into the air. That's over ten times as tall as your house.

•

In Iceland and New Zealand, hot underground water is used to make electricity. It's clean, cheap and it won't run out.

In places where volcanoes erupt, hot rocks sizzle away under the ground. The red-hot rocks heat up underground water until it reaches boiling point. Then the scalding hot water and steam shoot into the air as a ghastly, gushing geyser. Fancy one in your back garden?

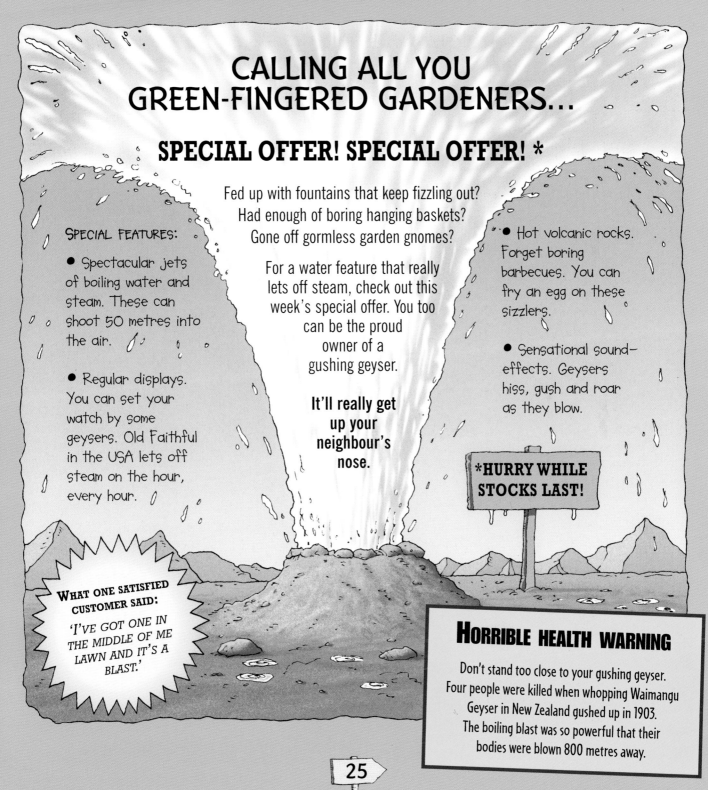

CALLING ALL YOU GREEN-FINGERED GARDENERS...

SPECIAL OFFER! SPECIAL OFFER! *

Fed up with fountains that keep fizzling out?
Had enough of boring hanging baskets?
Gone off gormless garden gnomes?

For a water feature that really lets off steam, check out this week's special offer. You too can be the proud owner of a gushing geyser.

It'll really get up your neighbour's nose.

SPECIAL FEATURES:

● Spectacular jets of boiling water and steam. These can shoot 50 metres into the air.

● Regular displays. You can set your watch by some geysers. Old Faithful in the USA lets off steam on the hour, every hour.

● Hot volcanic rocks. Forget boring barbecues. You can fry an egg on these sizzlers.

● Sensational sound-effects. Geysers hiss, gush and roar as they blow.

*HURRY WHILE STOCKS LAST!

WHAT ONE SATISFIED CUSTOMER SAID:
'I'VE GOT ONE IN THE MIDDLE OF ME LAWN AND IT'S A BLAST.'

HORRIBLE HEALTH WARNING

Don't stand too close to your gushing geyser. Four people were killed when whopping Waimangu Geyser in New Zealand gushed up in 1903. The boiling blast was so powerful that their bodies were blown 800 metres away.

WICKED WORLD WEATHER

If you're setting out on any journey, it pays to keep an eye on the weather. After all, you don't want to freeze to death if you're just popping out to the shops. But that's nothing compared to the wicked weather you're likely to meet on our whirlwind tour. Time to hang on to your hats. The going's about to get seriously stormy.

Wicked world climates

Climate is the kind of weather a place gets over years and years. And it all depends on how far away from the Equator and the odious oceans you are. Can't tell your temperate from your tropical? Muddled up mountain with monsoon? Why not get clued-up on climates with our latest Horrible Geography Guide.

Polar: Permanently freezing cold and icy, the parky poles are really cool. They're also the driest and windiest places on the whole planet. Brrr!

Tundra: A vast, flat stretch of icy wasteland around the nippy North Pole. There, the temperature only rises above freezing for a few measly months in summer.

Mediterranean: Places around the Mediterranean are cool and wet in winter, and hot and dry in summer. They're perfect for holidays because you're never far from the sea.

Mountain: The higher up a mountain you go, the chillier you'll feel. So, even close to the equator, many freaky peaks have ghastly glaciers on top.

Temperate: It's never horribly hot or cold in places between the poles and the tropics. There, you get warm summers and cool winters, with rain at any time.

Monsoon: Have your brolly handy in places with a monsoon climate. For half of the year, a dry wind blows. For the other half, it pours with rain.

Desert: Officially, bone-dry deserts get less than 250 mm of rain a year. They're also baking hot by day but can be teeth-chatteringly cold at night.

Tropical: Around the steamy equator, it's always hot and sticky, and woefully wet. It pours with rain almost every day, so expect to get completely soaked through.

26

SPINNING SEASONS

To muddle matters even more, you get different weather at different times of the year. That's because the seasons change as the Earth circles round the Sun.

1 The awesome Earth doesn't stand up straight. It tilts over to one side.

2 Every year, it travels around the Sun in an enormous loop.

3 At times, places tilt towards the Sun and are warm and sunny. Then it's spring and summer.

4 Meanwhile, other places tilt away from the Sun and are cold and dark. Then it's autumn and winter.

5 Places near the equator are always in the sun. They don't get spring, summer, autumn and winter. They just get hot, and even hotter!

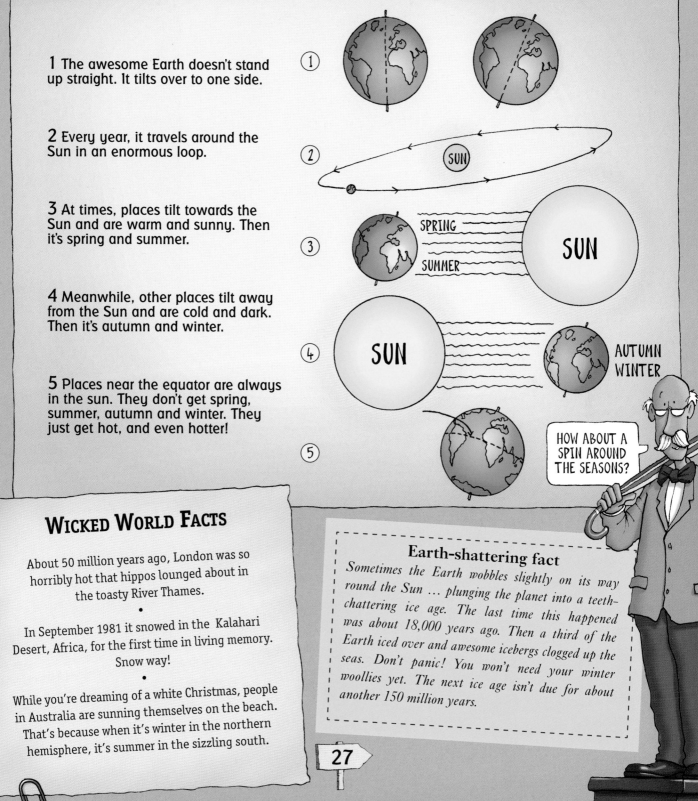

HOW ABOUT A SPIN AROUND THE SEASONS?

WICKED WORLD FACTS

About 50 million years ago, London was so horribly hot that hippos lounged about in the toasty River Thames.

•

In September 1981 it snowed in the Kalahari Desert, Africa, for the first time in living memory. Snow way!

•

While you're dreaming of a white Christmas, people in Australia are sunning themselves on the beach. That's because when it's winter in the northern hemisphere, it's summer in the sizzling south.

Earth-shattering fact

Sometimes the Earth wobbles slightly on its way round the Sun ... plunging the planet into a teeth-chattering ice age. The last time this happened was about 18,000 years ago. Then a third of the Earth iced over and awesome icebergs clogged up the seas. Don't panic! You won't need your winter woollies yet. The next ice age isn't due for about another 150 million years.

Some people like feeling the wind in their hair and getting wet through. Others find the cold rather bracing. Strange, but true. But if you want blue skies and hot sun on your hols, this weather report's not for you. It'll tell you about the wildest weather on the planet and which places you should AVOID AT ALL COSTS.

WORLD'S WORST WEATHER REPORT

1. Location: Yangtze River, China
Wild weather: **Flood 1998**
Torrential rains caused this raging river to burst its banks, drowning nearby villages. Over 2,000 people lost their lives and millions were left homeless.

2. Location: Ethiopia
Wild weather: **Drought 1981–85**
Lack of rain led to years of deadly drought, which killed crops and cattle. In the famine that followed, tens of thousands of people starved to death.

3. Location: Bangladesh
Wild weather: **Cyclone 1991**
In April, Cyclone 2B raced up the Bay of Bengal and struck the coast. Winds roared at 235 km/h, stirring up the sea into whopping 6-metre-high waves.

4. Location: Texas, USA
Wild weather: **Tornado 1997**
A twisting tornado 800 metres wide tore through the town of Jarrell, blasting a terrible trail of destruction and smashing the town into pieces.

5. Location: Durunka, Egypt
Wild weather: **Lightning 1994**
Lethal lightning hit a train carrying a cargo of fuel oil. The train exploded with a colossal bang, sparking off a fireball that set the nearby town on fire.

6. Location: Munich, Germany
Wild weather: **Hail 1984**
Rock-hard hailstones, as big as oranges, pelted the city, smashing roofs and windows, flattening crops and injuring hundreds of people.

7. Location: Australia
Wild weather: **Heatwave 1994**
In December, temperatures soared to a sweltering 44°C. Many people collapsed from heatstroke, and roads melted into gluey gum in the horrendous heat.

8. Location: Chicago, USA
Wild weather: **Snowstorm 1967**
In just ten days, 75 tonnes of snow fell and settled in massive drifts. The city ground to a halt. Some snow was sent south to sunny Florida as a present.

9. Location: Canada
Wild weather: **Deep freeze 1998**
A bone-chilling ice storm left three million people without power. Trees were snapped apart by the cold and collapsed under the weight of the ice.

10. Location: Egypt, Cyprus, Syria, Jordan
Wild weather: **Sandstorm 1988**
An especially savage sandstorm hurled tonnes of stinging sand into the air. Six people died in Cairo, Egypt, alone, and 250 were injured.

Postcard from Parky

Dear Gran

Well, here we are in Hawaii. And the weather's been woeful! Sorry if this postcard's a bit soggy but it's been raining buckets ever since we arrived. Apparently, it rains for about 335 days of the year here, making it the wettest place in the world. Wish someone had told me!

Love from Parky xxx

PS I've got loads of other postcards to show you when I get home.

MOUNT WAI-ALE-ALE, HAWAII

EUROPE

ASIA

AFRICA

AUSTRALIA

WICKED WORLD FACTS

Dallol, Ethiopia is a real hot spot, with an average temperature over a year of 34°4 C.

•

Wrap up warm if you're visiting Vostok in Antarctica. At -57.8°C, it's the coldest place on Earth.

•

Scared of the sound of thunder? Steer clear of Bogor, Java. It has over 300 thunderstruck days a year.

•

The windiest place in the world is breezy Commonwealth Bay, Antarctica. Here, ghastly gales can gust at over 300 km/h.

By the way, if you're planning a trip to the Eastern Sahara in Africa, pack plenty of sun cream. It's the sunniest place on Earth, with a sensational 4,300 hours of sunshine a year.

ODIOUS OCEANS

After all that wild and windy weather, how about a relaxing few days by the sea? Odious oceans cover two-thirds of the Earth so there's plenty of sea to, er, see. Hope you're ready to take the plunge. We're throwing you in at the deep end.

Spotter's guide to the sea bed

If you thought the silty sea bed was boringly flat, you're in for a surprise. In fact, there's a feast of fabulous features, just like on dry land. Only these fine features are covered in awesome amounts of sea water so most people have never seen them. Luckily you can dip into our special underwater Spotter's Guide. Right, Parky, dive in.

Sea-water recipe

Sea water's salty because – guess what – it's got salt in it. To make your own sea-water sample, try following this foul-tasting recipe.

SHARK BITE

You will need:
2 cupfuls of salt*
A bucket of warm-ish water
Large pinch of other chemicals (sulphate, magnesium, calcium and potassium, and so on)
Small pinch of gold (salt water contains other metals, too, but gorgeous gold's the most valuable)
A few fish (optional)

What to do:
1 Put the salt and other stuff in the water (except the gold and fish).
2 Stir until it dissolves.
3 Add the gold and the fish.

* **Note:** This salt's the same stuff you sprinkle on your food. But it doesn't come from a salt pot. Most of it comes from rocks on land, and rivers wash it into the sea.

Continental shelf:
Where the land slopes gently out to sea around the edges of the continents. (And nothing like a shelf you put a book on.)

Continental slope:
The end of the sloping shelf, where the sea bed falls steeply away down into the dark, dingy depths.

Continental rise:
A thick layer of murky mud and sand. It's washed down the slippery slope and makes a huge bump at the bottom.

Abyssal plains:
Frightfully flat plains that stretch across half of the sea floor. They're covered in a creepy carpet of ooze, made from the bodies of billions of dead sea creatures.

Wicked world oceans and seas

There are five odious oceans and lots of smaller seas. Actually, seas are parts of oceans, so it's all very confusing. See what I mean?

BEAUFORT SEA

BARENTS SEA

ARCTIC OCEAN (12,257,000 SQ KM)

BERING SEA

NORTH SEA

BERING SEA

CARIBBEAN SEA

MEDITERRANEAN SEA

ATLANTIC OCEAN (82,217,000 SQ KM)

ARABIAN SEA

RED SEA

SOUTH CHINA SEA

PACIFIC OCEAN

PACIFIC OCEAN (166,241,000 SQ KM)

INDIAN OCEAN (73,600,000 SQ KM)

CORAL SEA

WEDDELL SEA

SOUTHERN OCEAN (35,000,000 SQ KM)

TEACHER TEASER

See if your teacher's a salty old sea dog with this teaser. Which of these things have been found in a shark's stomach?
a) A dog, **b)** A car number plate, **c)** A sack of nails.

Answer: a), b) and **c)**! They're all been scoffed by a tiger shark. No wonder this greedy gut's nickname is 'garbage-can shark'. Its diet is rubbish.

WICKED WORLD FACTS

Millions of years ago, the water in the first oceans was like boiling hot vinegar. Odious.

•

The tallest wave ever seen was a whopping 34 metres high. Talk about making a splash.

•

Take a deep breath – over half the oxygen we breathe comes from minuscule ocean plants.

Seamount: A vast underwater volcano that towers a colossal kilometre or more from the sea bed. Thankfully, monster seamounts don't erupt any more.

Guyot: Similar to a seamount but without a pointy peak. A groovy guyot looks as if its head has been chopped right off. (Actually, it's been worn down by the washing of the waves.)

Mid-ocean ridge: Remember how the sea bed spreads? (See page 10 if you're not sure). This pushes up chunky chains of mountains and volcanoes down the middle of oceans.

Deep-sea trench: A giant gash in the sea floor. It happens when one plate of seabed plunges under another (see page 14 for an in-depth look).

Over a kilometre down in the ocean, the water's depressingly dark and cold. And it's horribly hard to find food. Amazingly, an astonishing number of animals feel right at home in these deadly depths. But how on Earth do they survive? Well, it helps if you dress the part. Wanda took a break from the world tour to drop in on this year's Daily Globe Fishy Fashion Awards. Here's her report:

FASHION AWARDS **DAILY GLOBE** *RESULTS!*

AWFUL ANGLER IN FISH FROCK SHOCK

3 1 2

Some of the best-dressed creatures in the deep sea took part in last night's ceremony. And what a glittering occasion it was.

With so many odious outfits on show, the judges had their work cut out. But they finally picked the winners.

IN 3RD PLACE:

Dressed from head to foot in bright red, the deep-sea prawn really cuts a dash. This dazzling outfit's not just pretty but practical, too. Red's a tricky colour to spot in the ocean depths, and many deep-sea fish are colour blind, so it's brilliant for camouflage.

IN 2ND PLACE:

The gulper eel's body is mostly made up of a massive mouth and a huge, extra-stretchy stomach. These allow the peckish eel to gulp down prey much larger than itself. It may not look very elegant but it's ideal for deep-sea living.

AND THE WINNER IS...

In 1st place: A unanimous decision. The judges had never seen anything like it before. The angler fish's fabulous fashion features include a blob of light dangling on a fin over its mouth. The light's made up of glowing bacteria and it's used like bait. Small fish mistake it for a tasty snack and swim straight into the angler's mega mouth. A truly eye-catching touch.

Back on dry land again, it's time for a short stroll along the cliff tops. All over the world, the crooked coast is being constantly battered by the wind, weather and waves. Horrible geographers call this erosion, and it eats away at the cliffs and rocks, carving the shoreline into shape. Now please stick closely to the path, everyone. We don't want you falling off the edge.

1. Headland: Let's start with that high bit of hard rock sticking out to sea. See the bit I mean with cliffs on either side? It's called a headland. Yes, you can look now.

2. Sea cave: If you look down, you'll see a couple of caves. They're made when waves wear away at cracks in the headland, carving them into holes. And they make brilliant hiding places for smugglers' loot.

3. Sea stack: You might want to move to your left. Watch out, that's your right. If the arch you're standing on collapses, you'll be left stranded out at sea, standing on top of a stack.

4. Blowhole: If waves smash through the roof of a sea cave, they spurt up through a blowhole (like the one on top of whale's head). Oooops! Right, I'm off for a sit down. That's given me quite a shock.

5. Arch: If you get two caves on either side of a headland, the sea sometimes punches a hole in between them. Anyone know what it's called? No? Oh dear, never mind – the answer's an arch.

CLIFF BY NAME, CLIFF BY NATURE!

WICKED WORLD FACTS

The highest sea cliffs are in Hawaii, but don't get too close to the edge – it's over a kilometre down.

•

Sand's made from tiny pieces of rock, coral and coal, smashed to smithereens by the wind and rain.

•

With over 90,000 km of shoreline, Canada boasts the most crooked coast. Nowhere on Earth can beat that.

ISOLATED ISLANDS & CRAZY CORAL REEFS

Where on Earth are we heading? To an isolated island, of course. Some people love islands, especially for holidays. Others think islands are just a load of boring rocks stuck out in the middle of the sea. What do you think? Before you make up your mind, here's some info about the two main island types.

Dear Gran

Here I am in Greenland. It's so far north, it's bitterly cold and icy all year round. Just like home. It's also the world's biggest island – almost four times the size of France. It's a continental island. Yep, it was once part of a continent (North America) but got cut off when the sea level rose and flooded the land in between. Must dash and have a nice, long dip in the freezing-cold sea.

Love from Parky xxx

GREENLAND, ARCTIC OCEAN

SUMATRA, INDONESIA

Dear Gran

Thanks for the sun cream. Since I got to Sumatra yesterday, it's been so horribly hot and steamy, especially when you're not used to it. Phew! Sizzling Sumatra's one of about 17,000 islands that make up the country of Indonesia. They're in the Indian Ocean so they're called oceanic islands. Get this: they're actually the tops of violent volcanoes that erupt under the sea. Oooh, what's that strange rumbling sound? I'm outta here.

Love from Parky xx

Before we leave the odious oceans, there's just time for one more quick boat trip. If you're after holiday snaps that will really impress your friends, a coral reef's the place to be. They're teeming with life and colour, and the busiest places in the sea.

Are you brave enough to build your own great barrier reef?

This is the biggest coral reef in the world and it's so massive that you can see it from the Moon. Here's Parky to demonstrate how you can make a Great Barrier Reef of your own.

What you need:
- 400 kinds of coral
- 1,500 kinds of fish
- 5,000 kinds of molluscs (they're creatures like giant clams, cone shells and odious octopuses)
- 500 kinds of seaweed
- 20 kinds of sea snakes
- 6 kinds of sea turtles
- Assorted whales, dolphins and porpoises
- 200 kinds of birds
- A shipwreck or two

What you do:
1 Find a warm, sunny sea for your reef (the north-east coast of Australia will do nicely).

2 Leave your coral to grow. Coral reefs are built by tiny sea creatures, called polyps. They're related to sea anemones and jellyfish. They live together in gigantic groups, billions of polyps strong. To protect their soft, squashy bodies, the polyps build hard, stony cases around themselves. When they die, the cases are left behind and build up the reef.

3 Wait for your reef to grow. But be warned. This could take time because coral only grows at about the same speed as your fingernails. The real Great Barrier Reef's about 2,300 km long and covers about 345,000 sq km. That's an awesome amount of reef and it's taken 18 MILLION YEARS to grow.

4 Add loads of animals. Coral reefs are home to thousands of sea creatures, including a third of all types of fish. In fact, they're so full of life, they're known as the gardens of the sea.

WICKED WORLD FACTS

All over the world, coral reefs are being ruined by pollution, fishing and mining.

•

Coral grows fastest in the evening, between about 6 and 8 pm when sea conditions are just right.

ROVING RIVERS

If messing about on rivers sounds restful, the next leg of our world tour could be just your cup of tea. But where on Earth do roving rivers start, and why do most of them end up running away to sea? To find out, Wanda set up an exclusive interview with a very old river, at his retirement home by the sea.

Wanda: Where were you born?

River: On the top of a mountain. I started off as a little spring. But it was all downhill from then on.

Wanda: What were you like in those early days?

River: Oh, always in a hurry - I was a real fast flower! And boy, was I strong! I could carry loads of heavy rocks - no problem at all.

Wanda: Wasn't all that rushing about horribly tiring?

River: Very. But I soon began to slow down. I ditched the rocks for mud and sand. They're much lighter, you see. Trouble is, I kept meandering off.

Wanda: Er, you what?

River: Well, instead of smashing straight through obstacles, I'd flow round them in giant loops.

Wanda: Hmm, I think I see what you mean. And what's life like now?

River: Oh, mustn't grumble. The land's nice and flat here so I can pootle along peacefully to the sea. Now, is that all, dear? I'm feeling rather sleepy. Zzzz.

Ten top roving rivers

Less than one per cent of all the water on Earth flows in roving rivers. Pathetic, eh? Even so, rivers pop up all over the world. Here's a map of ten of the longest.

NILE (6,695 KM)   OB-IRTYSH (5,410 KM)   LENA (4,400 KM)

AMUR (4,464 KM)

MISSISSIPPI (3,780 KM)

HUANG HE (4,672 KM)

AMAZON (6,439 KM)

MEKONG (4,184 KM)

CONGO (4,374 KM)

YANGTZE 6,376 KM)

DIPPY DELTAS: A spotters' guide

An old river is slow and sluggish. Near the sea, it runs out of energy and dumps its muddy load. Some of this makes new lumps of land, which the river has to flow round. Soon there's a mega maze of streams and islands called a delta. Here's Uncle Cliff with our Spotter's Guide to delta shapes…

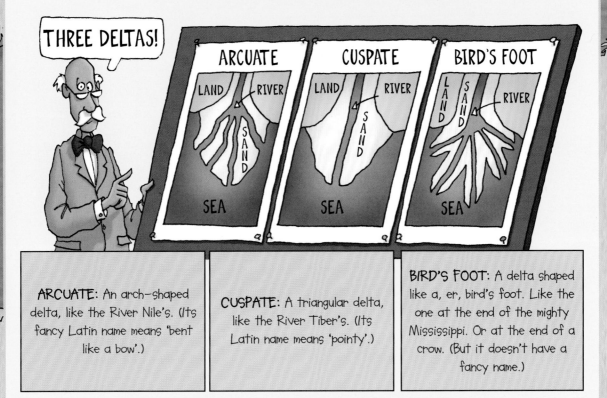

THREE DELTAS!

ARCUATE — CUSPATE — BIRD'S FOOT

ARCUATE: An arch-shaped delta, like the River Nile's. (Its fancy Latin name means 'bent like a bow'.)

CUSPATE: A triangular delta, like the River Tiber's. (Its Latin name means 'pointy'.)

BIRD'S FOOT: A delta shaped like a, er, bird's foot. Like the one at the end of the mighty Mississippi. Or at the end of a crow. (But it doesn't have a fancy name.)

Earth-shattering fact

The Grand Canyon, USA, is a ghastly gash in the Earth's surface. It's a steep-sided valley that's been carved out of the soft rock by the raging Colorado River. The Canyon's about 446 km long and a jaw-dropping 1.8 km deep. If you dare to make the descent, it'll take you two days by donkey.

WICKED WORLD FACTS

Every year, the Ob-Irtysh River ices over. That's great news for skaters but rubbish for the freezing fish.

•

The shortest river is D River in the USA. It's a record-breaking 37 metres short.

•

River water is horribly useful. You can drink it, water crops with it, fish in it, turn it into electricity and use it for getting from A to B.

oving rivers are full of surprises. Take waterfalls, for a start. This is where a river suddenly plummets over a band of hard rock that's blocking its way. Everyone ready for some thrills and spills?

Wicked waterfalls

If you're brave enough to open your eyes for a minute, here are the horrible details about how a wicked waterfall forms…

1 The river flows over a layer of hard rock with a layer of soft rock underneath.

2 It wears away the soft rock…

3 … until there's a step of hard rock left sticking out.

4 Then the river plunges right over the edge.

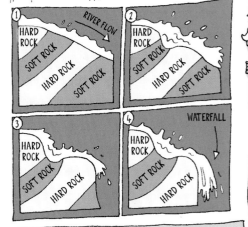

🌍 TEACHER TEASER 🌍

Send your teacher over the top with this teaser. What's the local name for the Victoria Falls in Africa?
a) The water that wails. **b)** The lion that roars.
c) The smoke that thunders.
Answer: c). The Victoria Falls plunge 108 metres over the Zambezi River. The water falls in such a rush it looks like smoke but it's actually trillions of minute water molecules. And all this falling water makes a thunderous booming sound.

WICKED WORLD FACTS

The way water wears rocks away is called erosion.

•

In 1859, sure-footed French daredevil Blondin walked across Niagara Falls … on a tightrope!

•

Enough water crashes over the Iguaçu Falls in South America to fill seven Olympic-sized swimming pools EVERY SECOND.

While rivers are busy wearing away valleys and waterfalls, water's also hard at work carving out caves underground. Warning: geography-lesson alert! What happens is this: rainwater's a weak acid, like very diluted lemon juice. It seeps into cracks in soft limestone rock and ever so slowly eats it away. Right now, you lot, mind your heads.

The inside story of a cave

Unless you've got super-sharp eyesight, you might find it tricky to track down an underground cave. So we've sent Wanda down to show you a cave's secret insides.

Sink hole: Where a stream plunges underground.

Pot hole: Like a sink hole but the stream's long gone.

Sump: A place where the cave roof's slumped.

Dry gallery: A passage worn away by a stream.

Flooded gallery: A passage that's still got its stream.

Chimney: A long drop worn away by a waterfall.

Cavern: Like a large room inside the cave.

WICKED WORLD FACTS

Some caves are colossal. The Sarawak Chamber in Borneo has got enough parking space for eight jumbo jets.

•

Most cave creatures are white. Well, what's the point of being snazzily dressed when no one can see you in the dark?

IDEAL CAVE MAGAZINE

Depressed by your cave's dull décor?

Tired of gazing at gloomy grey walls?

Give your clapped-out cave a make-over with the latest in cool cave chic.

Choose from our latest designer range of stalactites* and stalagmites*. Made from top-quality limestone, they're guaranteed to last for years.

Manufacturers' warning: Don't expect results overnight. It takes one of these beauties about 5,000 years to grow as long as your little finger.

MAKE SURE YOU PUT THEM IN THE RIGHT WAY UP. A STALACTITE GROWS DOWN FROM THE ROOF OF YOUR CAVE. A STALAGMITE GROWS UP FROM THE GROUND.

LEAKY LAKES

Back on the surface again, and there's just one watery world left to explore. No, you won't need a torch this time. The leaky lakes you'll be looking at are all above ground. Put simply, a lake's a large patch of water that fills a dip in the ground. So all lakes are damp and dippy, but they're also horribly different. Here are some notes Wanda jotted down for you about the main leaky lake types.

NOTES FROM MY TRAVELS
by Wanda
LEAKY LAKE TYPES

GLACIER LAKES: Fill dips gouged out by ancient glaciers in the last Ice Age. Like the Great Lakes in North America.

RIFT VALLEY LAKES: Long, snakey lakes lying in faults (colossal cracks) in the Earth's crust. Like Lake Tangyanika in East Africa.

CRATER LAKES: Collect in the craters of long-dead volcanoes. Like Crater Lake in the USA.

OX-BOW LAKES: Banana-shaped lakes that form when a meandering river gets cut off.

ARTIFICIAL LAKES: Where a dam's built across a river, stopping the flow. Like Lake Nasser in Egypt.

 TEACHER TEASER

See if your teacher's brain has sprung a leak with this teaser. Which of these lakes is the odd one out?
a) Caspian Sea. **b)** Dead Sea. **c)** Lake Superior.
Answer: c) Lake Superior's a freshwater lake. The other two are salty. That's why horrible geographers call them seas even though they're nowhere near the coast. Confusing, or what?

WICKED WORLD FACTS

Most leaky lakes get their water from rivers and rainfall.

•

In about 40,000 years, Lake Geneva in Switzerland will have been filled by mud dumped in it by the River Rhone.

•

Lake Chubb in Canada lies in a huge hollow left when a massive meteorite smashed into the Earth.

Leaky lake life story

Lakes don't last for ever. But don't worry, you won't miss a thing. Most lakes live for hundreds of thousands of years so there's plenty of time for snaps. Here's what happens as a leaky lake grows old.

1 A river dumps its load of mud and sand in the lake.

2 This builds up at one end, in a fancy fan shape.

3 The river dumps more mud and sand...

4 ... spreading the fan out further.

5 Slowly, the lake starts to shrink...

6 ... until it's completely filled in.

Top ten leaky lakes

Looking to locate a leaky lake? Here's a useful map of the world's top ten largest.

1. CASPIAN SEA (378,400 SQ KM)
2. LAKE SUPERIOR (82,100 SQ KM)
3. LAKE VICTORIA (69,484 SQ KM)
4. LAKE HURON (59,580 SQ KM)
5. LAKE MICHIGAN (57,700 SQ KM)
6. ARAL SEA (37,000 SQ KM)
7. LAKE TANGANYIKA (31,987 SQ KM)
8. LAKE BAIKAL (31,494 SQ KM)
9. GREAT BEAR LAKE (31,153)
10. LAKE NYASA (MALAWI) (28,877 SQ KM)

Fancy living by a lake? You won't be alone. Millions of people around the world already call leaky lakes home. So what do lakes have to offer that you can't get on dry land? For a start, there's plenty of water for drinking and washing behind your ears. Not to mention for fishing, swimming and messing about in boats. Still not convinced? Time to call the experts in.

BOGGY, LAKE & MARSH – ESTATE AGENTS
SPECIALISTS IN LAKE LOCATIONS

LAKE TITICACA, BOLIVIA/PERU

A superbly located lake. It's 4,000 metres up in the Andes Mountains so stunning views are guaranteed. The lake comes with its own handy supply of totora reeds. Brilliant for building boats or lakeside huts.

LAKE BAIKAL, RUSSIA

Deceptively deep and spacious (it's 1,742 metres at its deepest point). You could pour all five Great Lakes in and still have room to spare. An ideal spot for nature lovers. The lake's home to thousands of animals, including the only freshwater seal in the world.

LAKE MICHIGAN, USA

One of the five Great Lakes, it covers about 58,000 sq km. Choose from two major lakeshore cities – Chicago and Milwaukee. Cool Chicago's a major port and one of the world's top places for industry. Perfect if it's hustle and bustle you're after.

IF YOU'RE PLANNING A TRIP TO THE ARAL SEA IN CENTRAL ASIA, YOU'D BETTER GET A MOVE ON. THIS LEAKY LAKE'S VANISHING FAST. IT'S ALREADY SHRUNK TO HALF ITS FORMER SIZE, LEAVING FISHING BOATS AND ONCE-BUSY PORTS HORRIBLY HIGH AND DRY.

WICKED WORLD FACTS

The Dead Sea's so salty that it's impossible for swimmers to sink.

•

Wrap up warm if you're visiting Lake Vostok in Antarctica. This leaky lake's buried under 4 km of ice.

People aren't the only weird wildlife you'll find living near lakes. There's something far stranger lurking in the water. Feeling brave? You'll need to be. We're about to go monster hunting. Don't panic, you'll be quite safe…

MISSING!
HAVE YOU SEEN THIS MONSTER?

NAME: Loch Ness monster
AKA (also known as): NESSIE
LAST KNOWN ADDRESS: Loch Ness, Scotland

DISTINGUISHING FEATURES:
- Grey-green body
- Long snaky neck
- Little egg-shaped head
- Huge humps on its back

LAST SEEN: Hmm, good question. Thousands of monster-hunters say they've seen Nessie. They've even taken piccies (though some of these turned out to be monster fakes). Trouble is, no one's caught this mysterious creature yet. So it's still a mystery if it exists at all.

REWARD OFFERED FOR SAFE RETURN

Earth-shattering fact
The horrible truth is that Nessie has got the experts stumped. Some scientists reckon it's an ancient prehistoric reptile. Others wonder if it's a whopping whale or a monster fish. Or could it be people's eyes playing tricks on them. What do you think?

WICKED WORLD FACTS

Mysterious monsters have also been seen in lakes in Canada, the USA and Japan.

•

In a photo of Nessie from the 1950s, the humps turned out to be giant rocks.

DEADLY DESERTS

Seen enough water to last a lifetime? Looking forward to being back on dry land? Luckily, the next stop on our tour is one of the most parched places on the planet. So where on Earth are we heading? To the desperate desert, of course. But keep your water bottle handy. Unluckily, deserts are so desperately dry that you can easily die of thirst.

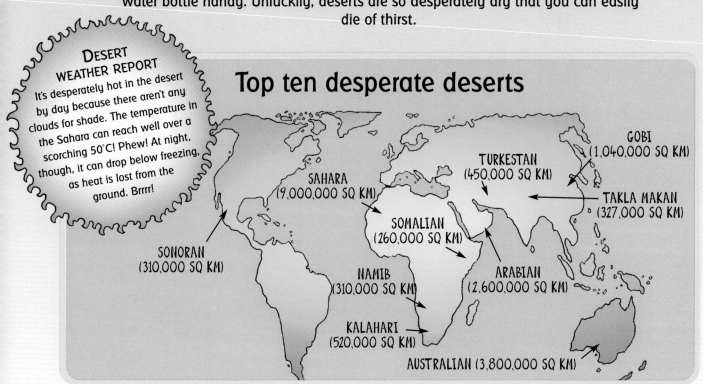

DESERT WEATHER REPORT
It's desperately hot in the desert by day because there aren't any clouds for shade. The temperature in the Sahara can reach well over a scorching 50°C! Phew! At night, though, it can drop below freezing, as heat is lost from the ground. Brrrr!

Top ten desperate deserts

GOBI (1,040,000 SQ KM)

TURKESTAN (450,000 SQ KM)

TAKLA MAKAN (327,000 SQ KM)

SAHARA (9,000,000 SQ KM)

SOMALIAN (260,000 SQ KM)

SONORAN (310,000 SQ KM)

NAMIB (310,000 SQ KM)

ARABIAN (2,600,000 SQ KM)

KALAHARI (520,000 SQ KM)

AUSTRALIAN (3,800,000 SQ KM)

Shifty sand dunes

Not all deserts are sandy. Some are rocky or covered in piles of pebbles. But if it's sand you're after, why not head for the scorching Sahara with Parky and watch a sand dune shift? Here's what happens:

1 THE SAND'S SHIFTED BY THE WIND. IT SLOWS DOWN IF IT HITS A ROCK OR A BUSH.
2 THEN IT SETTLES AND STARTS TO PILE UP.
3 IT BLOWS UP ONE SIDE...
4 ...UNTIL IT REACHES THE PEAK.
5 THEN IT FLOWS DOWN THE OTHER SIDE...
6 ...BURYING EVERYTHING IN ITS PATH.

① WIND BLOWS THIS WAY — SAND MOVES THIS WAY — ROCK

② WIND — ROCK

③ WIND — SAND MOVES THIS WAY — SLIP FACE

Horrible Holiday Guide:
DESERTS

All deserts are dry and dusty but they're also horribly different. Dip into our brand-new Horrible Holiday Guide to work out which sort of desert you're in:

Tropical deserts

Location: On either side of the equator.

Formation: Warm air cools and sinks. This creates a patch of high pressure that brings hot, dry weather.

Rain-shadow deserts

Location: On the sheltered side of some mountains.

Formation: Rain clouds form over mountains. But by the time they reach the other side, they've dumped all their rain.

Inland deserts

Location: In the middle of some continents.

Formation: They're so far from the sea, any rain's fallen long, long ago.

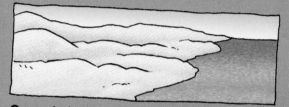

Coastal deserts

Location: Off the west coast of some countries.

Formation: Cold ocean currents cool the air blowing inland, so it's too dry to form rain clouds.

WICKED WORLD FACTS

Europe's the only continent that doesn't have deserts.

•

The sensational Sahara's as big as the whole of the USA.

•

The Empty Quarter in the Arabian Desert is a massive stretch of baking-hot sand.

TEACHER TEASER

Test your teacher's desert know-how with this teaser. What on Earth's a hammada?
a) A type of shifting sand dune. **b)** A rocky desert plain. **c)** A tool for banging in nails.
Answer: b) Hammada is the Arabic word for a rocky desert that's been stripped bare of sand and dust by the wind.

Deserts are such desperate places, it's a wonder anyone lives there at all. But despite the dreadful heat and drought, about 650 million people call deserts home. Hardy, or what? So how on Earth do these desert dwellers handle the harsh conditions? A few years ago, Wanda spent some time with the Bedouin people of the Arabian Desert and found out just how they keep their cool.

HORRIBLE HEALTH WARNING

Surviving in the desert is no picnic. Forget tucking into your sand-wiches. In the desert, food takes second place. You can go for weeks without eating but without water, you'd be dead in two days. To stay alive, you need to drink at least a bucket of water a day.

NOTES FROM MY TRAVELS
by Wanda

THE BEDOUIN

The Bedouin people mainly live in Arabia and North Africa. Their Arabic name is Bedu, which means 'people of the desert'.

The Bedouin are nomads, which means they're constantly on the move. They shift from place to place in search of food and water for themselves and their animals.

With all that moving, they need a home that's easy to put up and take down and that fits neatly on the back of a camel. And what could be better than a nice, snug tent made from camel's hair or sheep's wool?

When it comes to desert dress, the Bedouin know what to wear. And keeping cool's what counts. Their loose, flowing robes are ideal for letting air circulate and their long headdresses keep the sand and sun out.

The Bedouin are famous for their hospitality. They'll always give guests a meal and a place to stay. But watch your manners. Turn down a cup of coffee and you'll offend the whole family.

It's not just horribly hardy humans who live in the desperate desert. Hundreds of plants and animals have found clever ways of finding water and staying cool. Trouble is, some of them are just too bloomin' clever for their own good. We sent Parky to investigate.

Are you brave enough to get water out of a frog?

A daring desert frog from Australia has an ingenious way of surviving dry spells. It stores water in its body and sits it out underground until it rains. So what on Earth has this freaky frog got to do with you? Imagine you're in the desert and you've run out of water. Ever heard the saying 'getting blood out of a stone'? Well, what about 'getting water out of a frog'? Here's what you have to do:

1 Stamp your feet on the ground. (The frog thinks this sounds like thunder and that it's going to rain.)

2 When the frog croaks, dig it up quickly.

3 Hold the frog over your mouth and give it a good squeeze!

Yes, I know it sounds horribly cruel and heartless, but for local desert people these thirst-quenching frogs are life-savers. If you're going to try this at home, ask the frog's permission first.

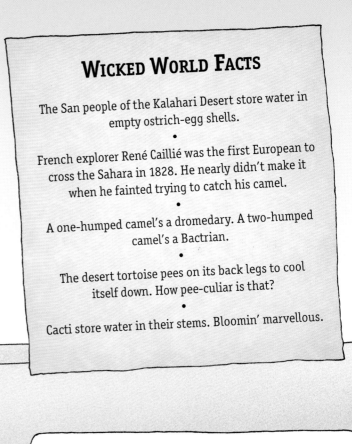

WICKED WORLD FACTS

The San people of the Kalahari Desert store water in empty ostrich-egg shells.

•

French explorer René Caillié was the first European to cross the Sahara in 1828. He nearly didn't make it when he fainted trying to catch his camel.

•

A one-humped camel's a dromedary. A two-humped camel's a Bactrian.

•

The desert tortoise pees on its back legs to cool itself down. How pee-culiar is that?

•

Cacti store water in their stems. Bloomin' marvellous.

NEVER LEAVE HOME WITHOUT A CAMEL. OK, SO THEY'RE TERRIBLY BAD-TEMPERED AND TEND TO SPIT. (THAT'S PROBABLY WHY SOME DESERT PEOPLE USE LAND ROVERS INSTEAD.) BUT THEY'RE BRILLIANTLY ADAPTED TO DESERT LIFE AND CAN WALK MILES WITHOUT WATER OR FOOD. AND IF YOUR CAMEL'S PLAYING UP, TRY THIS BEDOUIN REMEDY. POUR SPIT DOWN ITS NOSE TO GET RID OF THE EVIL SPIRITS.

GROOVY GRASSLANDS

With the desperate desert behind us, our next stop should be a walk in the park. To prove grass isn't just the boring, green stuff that grows in gardens, I've lined up a quick fact-finding trip to the groovy grasslands. Is the grass always greener? You're about to find out with our quick Grasslands Guide.

Horrible Geography Guide:
GRASSLANDS

There are two main types of groovy grasslands. But you'll need a big back garden if you're planning to grow one at home. Between them, these vast, grassy plains cover about one-fifth of the Earth.

Tropical grasslands

Tropical grasslands mostly grow near the equator. Here the weather's baking hot all year round. But there's also a dry season when the plains are parched, and a rainy season when they burst into bloom again.

Location: Africa; Southeast Asia; India; Australia

Temperate grasslands

Temperate grasslands grow in the middle of some continents. Here summers are hot and dry but winter temperatures can plummet to a perishing −40°C in the bone-chilling wind.

Location: South Africa; South America; Russia; North America

IF YOU'RE EXPLORING A GRASSLAND, KEEP YOUR WITS ABOUT YOU. WITH NOTHING BUT GRASS FOR MILES AROUND, IT'S EASY TO GET LOST. DEAD LOST. IN THE SIXTEENTH CENTURY, SOME INTREPID SPANISH EXPLORERS SET OFF TO RIDE ACROSS THE NORTH AMERICAN PRAIRIE. BY THE TIME THEY REACHED THE OTHER SIDE, ONE MAN AND TWO HORSES WERE MISSING.

 TEACHER TEASER

Really get up your teacher's nose with this teaser. Which of these is the odd one out?
a) Rice. **b)** Wheat. **c)** Bamboo.
Answer: Sorry, trick question. Believe it or not, they're ALL kinds of grass. The other 9,997 kinds of grass include barley, maize and sugar cane. Has your teacher grass-ped all that?

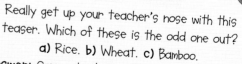

Groovy global grasslands

Guess what? Yep, horrible geographers have thought up lots of fancy-sounding names for grasslands in different parts of the world. What on Earth's wrong with calling them plain grasslands? Anyway, here's the pick of the bunch.

PRAIRIE
(NORTH AMERICA)

STEPPES
(ASIA)

SAVANNAH
(AFRICA)

VELDT
(SOUTH AFRICA)

RANGELANDS
(AUSTRALIA)

PAMPAS; LLANOS; CERRADOS
(SOUTH AMERICA)

HORRIBLE HEALTH WARNING

Groovy grasslands all over the world are in grave danger. Horrible humans are digging them up to make room for farms and grazing land. Trouble is, if the land's used again and again, it quickly gets worn out. In the 1930s, farmers in the USA ploughed up the prairie to grow wheat. But the worn-out soil soon turned to dust and blew away in the wind.

WICKED WORLD FACTS

The first grasslands grew about 20 million years ago when the world's weather turned much drier than it had been previously.

•

Grasslands grow in places where there's not enough rain for a forest to sprout, but it's not dry enough for a desert.

•

The largest wheat field ever was about the size of 20,000 soccer pitches.

So, apart from getting lost in, what on Earth's so bloomin' great about grass? You might be surprised. Someone who knows the answer is our very own Uncle Cliff. When he's not giving serious scientific talks, he likes nothing better than pootling about in his garden.

GROOVY GRASSLAND GROWING TIPS

Forget boring roses and dull old dahlias. They're not a patch on grass. It's my favourite plant in the world. So I thought I'd give you my three top tips for keeping your grassland in tip-top condition. Your friends will go green with envy – mark my words.

- Keep your grass cut nice and short. There are plenty of animals to do this so you won't need a lawnmower. The great thing about grass is it keeps on growing no matter how much it's nibbled.

- If your grassland catches fire, don't panic. Grass is horribly hardy. It'll soon grow back again. In fact, the fire might do you a favour. It burns off any old, dead veg and lets the new, green shoots sprout. Lovely.

- Keep your hanky handy. Grasses are flowering plants and the pesky pollen (that's the dust-like stuff flowers make seeds from) might set off a stinking dose of hayfever. Aaatchooo! (Ok, so this isn't strictly a top tip but you'll thank me for it, you really will.)

WICKED WORLD FACTS

Grassland trees, called baobabs, store water in their big, bulging trunks.

•

Tasty pasta's made from durum wheat, and that's a kind of grass!

Earth-shattering fact
On the grassland, you might think having a black and white coat would make you stick out like a sore thumb. But a zebra's stripy coat actually makes it tricky for a lion to pick out in a crowd. Cool.

Grass isn't just good news for cows. Thousands of grassland animals munch grass for every meal. And get this. To avoid a feeding frenzy, they each eat different parts of the grass plants.

Zebras eat the tops, while wildebeest munch the stems. Gazelles like to guzzle grass shoots. But some other grassland greedy-guts have terrible table manners…

HORRIBLE FEEDING HABITS

Vultures fly around in gangs on the look-out for a lion's leftovers. Dead zebra's a favourite. Then they drop in for dinner. They've got short, sharp beaks for picking bones clean, and bare heads and necks so their feathers don't get soaked in blood. Foul.

Dung beetles eat poo! It's disgusting but true. They use their back legs to roll up balls of animal dung. Then they bury the balls underground. Over the next few days, the beetles keep sneaking back for a smelly snack.

Guess what a **giant anteater's** favourite food is? No, it isn't sausage and chips. It's ants, of course. But this grassland greedy-guts needs an awful lot of ants to fill it up. So it creeps up on an ants' nest and rips it open with its claws. Then it flicks its long tongue in and out, slurping up hundreds of ants with each sticky lick.

Grass and plants are terrifically tough to digest. So some animals, like **antelopes**, have a sickening way of coping. Food stays in their stomach for a few hours while it's softened by stomach juices. Then it's sicked up again for another chew!

WICKED WORLD FACTS

Elephants have enormous appetites. They eat over a third of a tonne of grass a day.

•

Ostriches are too blooming big to fly. But they can run as fast as a galloping horse. Giddy-up, birdy.

STEAMY RAINFORESTS

Next stop on our intrepid tour are the steamy rainforests. Ha, ha. Rainforests are home to at least half the world's kinds of plants and animals. So be sure to have your cameras ready for a snap. But you'll also see millipedes the size of small rocks, and plants that like to munch meat. It really is a jungle out there.

RAINFORESTS: A spotters' guide

All rainforests are lush, green and steamy so it's easy to get them mixed up. But there are different kinds of rainforest, depending on where they grow. Here's a quick spotters' guide for you to leaf through.

Lowland rainforests
Where found: Low-lying land along the equator.
Appearance: Packed with mostly evergreen trees (they keep their leaves all year round).

Montane rainforests
Where found: On tropical mountain slopes.
Appearance: Cooler and damper because they're higher up. Usually covered by cloud.

Mangrove forests
Where found: Along tropical coasts.
Appearance: Muddy swamps at river mouths. Trees have long, tangled roots for gripping the mud.

Flooded forests
Where found: Along tropical river banks.
Appearance: Spend months covered in 15 metres of water when a river bursts its banks.

RAINFOREST WEATHER REPORT

It's hot and steamy in the rainforest whatever time of year you go. That's because you're close to the equator, where the Sun's rays are seriously strong. And it pours with rain almost every day, so expect to get soaking wet.

Earth-shattering fact
By far the biggest rainforest blooms along the banks of the Amazon River in steamy South America. It covers six million sq km. That's twice as big as the whole of India. Awesome!

Luscious layers

Blooming rainforest trees grow in layers, depending on how tall they are. Hope Parky doesn't mind heights.

1 Emergents: The tallest trees in the forest. Their tops poke up at heights of 60 metres and more. Yikes, it's a long way down.

2 Canopy: A luscious layer of treetops about 30–40 metres above ground. Like a leafy forest roof. Most of the forest's plants and animals live here so you're never alone.

WICKED WORLD FACTS

In a patch of rainforest the size of a soccer pitch, you might find 200 different kinds of tree.

•

Most rainforest animals live in the canopy, so it gets pretty crowded up there.

•

Some rainforest plants don't bother with soil. They perch on tree branches, dangling their roots in the air which is full of the moisture they need to survive.

3 Understorey: Spindly saplings and small trees, covered in creepers and vines. So it's easy to get in a tangled up. Help! I'm stuck.

Rainforests mostly grow in three massive chunks – in South America, Southeast Asia and Africa. In case you haven't got a rainforest at home, here's a map to help you find your closest.

4 Forest floor: A damp and gloomy tangle of mosses, ferns, fungi and piles of old, dead leaves. And creepy crawlies. Eek! What was that rustling sound?

53

Warning! If insects give you the creeps, you might like to skip the next bit. You see, the most common rainforest creatures aren't cheeky monkeys or twittering birds. They're creepy **CREEPY CRAWLIES!** In fact, more insects live in the rainforest than anywhere else on Earth. Fancy meeting some of these ugly bugs?

UGLY BUG BEAUTY CONTEST

Highly commended
A special mention has to go to this seriously strange fly. Its beady eyes are out on stalks but no one's got the foggiest why. They might be used to attract female flies. Well, they say love is blind.

WINNER
The winner of this year's contest is the giraffe-necked weevil from Madagascar. With its stumpy, red body and long, sticky neck, all the judges agreed this weird weevil is no oil painting.

Runner-up
The peanut bug from South America almost won for its ludicrous looks. Its huge false head looks dead scary (if you find peanuts frightening) but in fact this ugly bug's totally harmless.

A PARTICULARLY IRRITATING RAINFOREST INSECT IS THE MADDENING MOSQUITO. TO STOP A MOSSIE BITING YOU, TRY SLAPPING SOME RANCID ALLIGATOR FAT ON YOUR SKIN. IT SMELLS TERRIBLE BUT IT WORKED A TREAT FOR ACE EXPLORER ALEXANDER VON HUMBOLDT (1769-1859) ON HIS EXPEDITION UP THE AMAZON.

Rainforests are crammed full of riches for horrible humans to use. If you're chomping a choccie bar while you're reading this, you're using one of them already. Chocolate is made from beans from the cocoa tree that blooms in the rainforest. So what else might be on your rainforest shopping list?

RAINFOREST RICHES SHOPPING LIST

FRUIT AND VEG
Choose from bananas, pineapples, avocadoes, oranges, lemons and aubergines. Yep, they all grow on rainforest trees.

NUTS
Try some crunchy Brazil nuts (even if it isn't Christmas). You can also get peanuts and cashews.

GINGER BICCIES
Ginger's one of hundreds of scrummy spices found in the rainforest. It gives these biccies their yummy taste.

HOUSE PLANTS
Stuck for a pressie for your mum's birthday? Pick a rainforest bloomer. African violets, cheese plants and nasturtiums all originally came from the rainforest.

PERFUME
Can't find the perfect plant? Don't worry. Try a sniff-tacular scent made from fragrant rainforest flowers instead!

HORRIBLE HEALTH WARNING

Rainforests are being destroyed at such a rate, that they might all be gone in 30 to 50 years' time. So why are the forests for the chop? It's mostly for the very valuable timber that comes from rainforest trees. But also to clear land for homes, farms, mines and cattle ranches. And the trouble is, it takes the forests thousands of years to grow back.

WICKED WORLD FACTS

About a third of all rainforest creatures are ... awesome ants.

•

About a quarter of the medicines we take when we're ill come from rainforest plants.

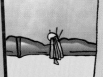

WILD WOODLANDS

Just when you thought you were out of the woods, there's some more fabulous forest blooming, sorry, looming. Welcome to the world's wild woodlands. Don't worry, they'll soon start to grow on you.

Horrible Holiday Guide:
WOODLANDS

Apart from steamy rainforests, there are two main kinds of woodlands. Worried about barking up the wrong tree? Here's our wicked woodland guide.

Name: BOREAL (NORTHERN) FORESTS

Location: Across the far north of Europe, Asia and North America

Forest features:

• They're also called the taiga, which is Russian for 'dark, mysterious woodland'. Spooky.

• The trees are mainly conifers, like pine, larch, redwood, fir and spruce. They're also evergreen.

• They grow close together so the forest floor's gloomy and dark.

• Among the woodland wildlife you might meet are bears, wolves, beavers, lynx and porcupines.

Name: TEMPERATE FORESTS

Location: In patches all over the world

Forest features:

• The trees are mainly broad-leaved trees, like oak, beech, elm, hazel, maple and silver birch.

• They're mostly deciduous. This means they lose their leaves in winter, then they bloom again in spring.

• These forests are quite light and airy because the trees grow further apart.

• Woodland wildlife includes ladybirds, deer, wild boar, badgers and woodpeckers.

Spot the conifer

Wild woodland trees have clever ways of coping with the weather where they live. Forget boring spot-the-difference. Can you spot the conifer?

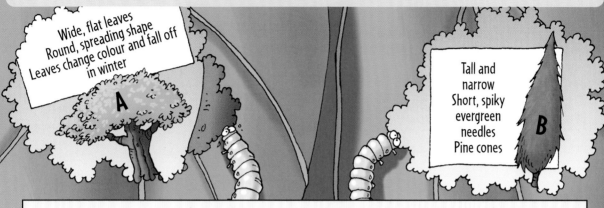

Wide, flat leaves
Round, spreading shape
Leaves change colour and fall off in winter

A

Tall and narrow
Short, spiky evergreen needles
Pine cones

B

Answer: Tree B) Cold-weather conifers have to be hardy. Their clever cone shape lets snow slide off their branches so they don't break under its weight. And instead of leaves, they have waxy needles, which are brilliant at sealing water in. But bloomin' broad-leaved trees also have a few tricks up their leaves, sorry, sleeves. Their wide leaves and spreading shape are designed to catch lots of sunlight which they use to make food. And they lose their leaves in winter to save energy.

Wild world woodlands

Wondering which wild woodland to wander along to? Here's a map to help you make up your mind.

Boreal (northern) forests

Temperate forests

WICKED WORLD FACTS

The paper used to make this book probably came from a chopped-down conifer.

•

The tallest trees are giant redwoods. To climb one of these beauties, you'd need a ladder over 100 metres tall.

•

The Christmas tree you cover in lights and tinsel is a cool Yule conifer.

WOODLAND WEATHER REPORT

Boreal forests grow in the bracing far north. Summers are short and cool but winters are f-f-freezing. The temperature can drop below -60°C and it's seriously snowy. Temperate forests grow in places with warm summers and mild winters, and where it's never horribly hot or cold.

Every blooming tree in the forest is home to hundreds of wild woodland animals. You'll find 300 different kinds of insects alone living up an oak tree. But if you were a woodland creature, which bit of tree would you choose as home?

ROOT, BRANCH & TWIG – ESTATE AGENTS
HELPING YOU FEEL AT HOME WITH NATURE

FOR SALE

A selection of exclusive oak-tree homes. Superbly situated in a leafy forest glade

 Branches: Perfect perches for owls. Double up as bases for hunting prey and handy for a quick kip. (Also suitable for squirrels and bats.)

 Leaves: Not only a lovely spot to live in but you won't have to go out to eat. Butterflies, pick a leaf to lay your eggs on. Then your caterpillars will have plenty of lunch to munch. (Our most popular home by far, with over 250,000 leaves for sale.)

 Bark: Plenty of room for you beetles to burrow and lay your eggs. Then your grubs can have bark for breakfast. (Watch out for the neighbours, though. They might be woodpeckers.)

 Trunk: A dream home for woodpeckers. Use your sharp beak to drill for grubs or to hollow yourself out a nice cosy hole for a nest.

 Leaf buds: Brilliant for you gall wasps to lay your eggs in. You won't even have to look after them. A little swelling (gall) will grow around each grub for it to feed on.

 Roots: These basement homes make great dens for shrews and voles. De-luxe apartments with built-in tunnels and burrows also available for badgers.

FOR SALE

Special Offer
Buy now and get a lifetime supply of acorns. **Free.**

Our guarantee:
Oak trees are built to last and can live for up to 450 years. They're also seriously sturdy so they won't blow down in the wind. (Usually.)

The nippy northern forests are tough places to live. They're bitterly cold in winter, and finding food can take days. But despite the harsh conditions, people have called these forests home for thousands of years. How on Earth do they survive? Here are some notes Wanda jotted down when she visited the Evenk people of Siberia.

NOTES FROM MY TRAVELS
by Wanda
THE EVENK

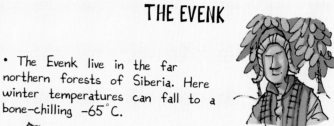

• The Evenk live in the far northern forests of Siberia. Here winter temperatures can fall to a bone-chilling -65°C.

• The Evenk live by herding reindeer. In fact, their name means 'people who run faster than reindeer'. Once a month, they pack up camp and set off to find fresh lichen for their reindeer to graze on.

• Reindeer are horribly useful. They pull the Evenks' sledges and carry heavy loads. Luckily, they've got big, broad hooves that don't sink in the snow.

• But that's not all. To survive the freezing winter, the Evenk need to wrap up warm. Guess what they make winter clothes from? Yep, reindeer skin, of course. Reindeer-skin boots, lined with reindeer-hair socks, are ideal for keeping their toes toasty warm.

• The Evenk also rely on reindeer for most of their food. They like to munch on reindeer meat and cheese, washed down with reindeer milk or blood. And for extra vitamins, they chew on the half-digested contents of the reindeer's stomach. Fancy dropping in for tea?

PS: The Evenk also rely on reindeer for most of their food. They like to munch on reindeer meat and cheese, washed down with reindeer milk or blood. And for extra vitamins, they chew on the half-digested contents of the reindeer's stomach. Fancy dropping in for tea?

WICKED WORLD FACTS

Some moths roll themselves in oak leaves to hide from hungry birds.

•

You can tell trees apart by their bark patterns. Oak bark is rough and groovy.

COLD POLES

Reckon the northern forests are plenty nippy enough for you? Well, get ready for a fearfully frosty surprise. For our next stop, we're off to the p-p-perishing poles. They're the parkiest places on the planet, and they're covered in miles and miles of snow and ice. Think you'll be able to keep your cool?

Polar weather report

It's bitterly cold at the poles. Get this – at the South Pole, the average winter temperature's a teeth-chattering -60°C. It's warmer at the North Pole, though it's still a chilly -30°C. And to make matters worse, it's also horribly windy, with gales howling at speeds of over 300 km/h and whipping the snow up into blinding blizzards. No wonder you're getting cold feet. What's that? Why are the perishing poles so cold? It's a very good question. Here's a handy diagram.

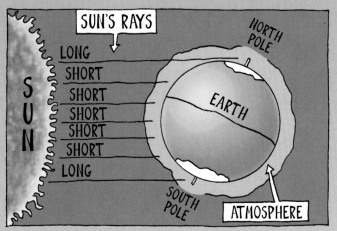

Perishing polar cold

The poles are so bitterly cold because the Earth's surface is curvy. How on Earth does this curve cause the Earth to catch cold? What happens is this. Because of the Earth's curve, the Sun's rays hit the poles at a wide angle. They're spread out over a wide area, which makes them woefully weak. What's more, the roving rays have to take a longer route through the Earth's atmosphere. On the way, they lose heaps of heat. The ice at the poles also helps them keep their cool. Light colours reflect heat away while dark colours soak it up. So, most of the sunlight that reaches the poles is reflected straight back into space by the white ice.

WICKED WORLD FACTS

There's no land at the North Pole, only frozen ocean.

•

Antarctica's actually a colossal ice-covered continent.

FIVE FROSTY FACTS

1 A massive sheet of ice covers 99 per cent of Antarctica. In places, this gigantic ice slice is a staggering 5 km thick. And it's so heavy, the land's sunk beneath its weight.

2 Every year, thousands of icebergs break away from slippery ice sheets and glaciers and float out to sea. Baby bergs are about as big as pianos. The biggest berg ever seen was the size of Belgium! By the way, icebergs make brilliant penguin diving boards.

3 Two-thirds of an iceberg lies underwater, which makes it hard for ships to spot. In 1912, the luxury liner, RMS *Titanic*, hit a berg in the North Atlantic and sunk with the loss of 1,490 lives.

4 A bit further north, the freezing Arctic Ocean is covered in ice almost all year round. This sea ice is about 5 metres thick.

5 In places, the Arctic sea ice breaks into bits that drift on the wind and ocean currents. These pieces make perfect perches for polar bears, as they float out to sea in search of seals.

Perishing polar map

To pop in on the perishing poles, you'll need to go to the very ends of the Earth. They're at either end of the Earth's axis (that's an imaginary line running from top to bottom). The area around the North Pole is called the Arctic. Antarctica is the area around the South Pole. Got all that?

> YOU MIGHT BUMP INTO A POLAR BEAR AT THE NORTH POLE BUT YOU WON'T FIND ANY PENGUINS. WE ONLY HANG OUT AROUND THE SOUTH POLE.

Earth-shattering fact
Strictly speaking, icy Antarctica counts as a desert. Even though it's so cold. With a measly 50 mm of rain a year, it's as dry as a load of old bones.

Congratulations! You've come this far and you haven't frozen to death yet. But have you really got the hang of perilous polar living?

Try this quick quiz to see if you'd survive. All the answers are based on how the local Inuit people traditionally coped with the icy Arctic cold.

COULD YOU BE A POLAR EXPLORER?

1 A thick woolly jumper is all you'll need to keep you toasty and warm. YES/NO?

2 Muklucks are warm, furry boots made from sealskin. YES/NO?

3 In a snowstorm, stand your ground until the blizzard blows over. YES/NO?

4 You've caught a seal for supper. But don't eat its intestines. YES/NO?

5 To get from A to B quickly, hitch some sausage dogs to your sledge. YES/NO?

ANSWERS:

1 NO. You need to wear lots of layers of clothes to trap warm air next to your skin. They'll also let sweat escape so it doesn't freeze on your skin.

2 YES. But did you know the sealskin is soaked in wee overnight to get it clean?

3 NO. The best thing to do in a snowstorm is to make a shelter from snow. Snow's brilliant for building with because it traps heat.

4 NO. The only bit of a seal you can't eat is its ghastly gall bladder. Dried intestines are a delicacy.

5 YES AND NO. It's true that travelling by dog sledge is the best way to get about. But you won't get far with sausage dogs. Hitch up some hardy huskies instead.

So how did you do? Award yourself ten points for each right answer.

SCORE:

Score 0–20: Oh dear! You won't last long at the parky poles. At this rate, you'll freeze to death before you could say 'Polar bear!'

Score 30–40: You've got what it takes to survive at the poles, if you keep your wits about you. But hang on ... how did that sausage dog manage to sneak in there?

Score 50: You'll make a brilliant polar explorer and you'll be living like a local in no time. So let's hope you like mashed seal's brain because that's what you've got for tea.

HORRIBLE HEALTH WARNING

No one lives in Antarctica permanently. It's just too perishing cold. But thousands of suffering scientists travel there to work. They mostly live on research stations, with their own living quarters, kitchens, hospitals, gyms and horrible science labs.

If you're planning another trip to the parky poles, you'd better get your skates on. The poles may look like useless lumps of ice, but there's lots of stuff underneath you could put to good use. From oil and minerals, to fish and fur seals, the poles are packed with riches. Trouble is, horrible humans are so busy getting them out that they're putting the poles in peril.

HORRIBLE HOLIDAYS
are not proud to present their poles-in-peril tour

Hurry while the poles last

For a holiday you might want to forget, try our poles-in-peril tour. But watch out for the piles of litter and rotten rubbish dumped by passing tourists. And mind the miles of polar coast polluted by oil spilled when tankers run aground.

TODAY'S SPECIAL OFFER!
Fancy going toothfish fishing? Don't bother. There probably aren't any toothfish left. The toothfish's tasty meat makes it a valuable catch. But in the Southern Ocean, huge numbers are being caught illegally. Trouble is, it takes a toothfish about 30 years to be fully grown. And so many fish are being caught, stocks don't have time to catch up.

A NOTE FROM YOUR TOUR OPERATOR:
We can't guarantee you'll see anything. Especially if you book late. According to some scientists, humans are making the Earth so warm, the poles are melting before our eyes.

WICKED WORLD FACTS

One plan is to turn the whole of Antarctica into a whopping World Park. Wicked.

•

There are strict rules to stop real-life tourists making a mess and disturbing polar wildlife*.

*AND THAT MEANS ME!

WICKED
WORLD COUNTRIES

While you're thawing out after your bone-chilling trip to the poles, here's a horrible geography question. How many countries are there in the whole wicked world? Go on, have a wild guess? Give up? You're not alone. Even ghastly geographers can't agree. Most of them reckon on 192, give or take one or two.

① **Biggest!** Measuring a massive 17,075,400 sq km, Russia's the world's largest country. In fact, it's so blooming big, it doesn't all fit into one continent but stretches across two – Europe and Asia.

② **Smallest!** You could fit the Vatican City in Italy into Russia over 38 MILLION times! The headquarters of the Roman Catholic Church, it's also the world's smallest country, covering just 0.44 sq. km. So it's just as well no more than 1,000 people live there.

③ **Most people!** More people live in China than in any other country in the world. China's home to about 1.3 billion people – that's about a fifth of everyone on Earth. Luckily, China's colossal (9,326,410 sq km) so there's plenty of room for everyone.

④ **Richest!** The world's richest country is Luxembourg. This tiny country's tucked away between France, Germany and Belgium, but it's grown mega-rich from making iron and steel. With all this lovely dosh, it's lucky that Luxembourg's also famous for having loads of banks.

⑤ **Poorest!** Mozambique in Africa shares the terrible title of the world's poorest country with Somalia. The average person there earns about one hundredth of the salary of an average person in cash-rich Luxembourg.

⑥ **Newest!** Montenegro is the world's newest country. It became a country in 2006 after splitting from Serbia.

⑦ **Most space!** If you like wide, open spaces, Mongolia's the place to be. With only two people for each square kilometre, it's the least crowded country in the world. Pining for some peace and quiet? Mongolia's got bucketloads.

STARS AND BARS! Because it's, er, starry and stripy, the USA's flag's known as the Stars and Stripes. There are 13 stripes, one for each state that existed in 1777 when the flag was first used. And there are 50 stars, one for each state today.

STARRY SKIES! There are more stars on the Brazilian flag, twinkling like the night sky over the city of Rio de Janeiro. There is a motto around the middle of the blue globe that means 'Order and Progress'. The rest of the flag stands for the Amazon rainforest (the green bit) and Brazil's wealth in gold (the yellow bit).

UNION JACK! The United Kingdom's world-famous flag is called the Union Jack. It's made up of the crosses of St George, St Andrew and St Patrick, the patron saints of England, Scotland and Ireland. (By the way, this jack's the name of a small ship's flag, and not the boy you sit next to in class.)

AWESOME ASIA

If it's the trip of a lifetime you're after, why not check out the crazy continents? You could start off in Asia. With deserts, volcanoes and freaky peaks, it's a wicked place to hang out. But before you get going, why not sneak a peak at the itinerary* for your intrepid tour? It's so incredibly action-packed, your feet won't touch the ground. Welcome to the Awesome Asian Adventure…

Day 1: Caspian Sea
First stop is the Caspian Sea. It covers a colossal 378,400 sq. km and is the world's largest lake. It's famous for caviar, a delicacy made from exotic fish eggs. Anyone fancy a spoonful on toast?

Day 2: Dead Sea
Our next stop's the spooky Dead Sea between Israel and Jordan. It's not really a sea at all but a salty, inland lake. Actually, it's so seriously salty that nothing can live in it. That's why it's called 'dead'.

Day 3: Red Sea
We spend the next few days of our tour relaxing by the Red Sea. It's part of the Indian Ocean and splits Asia from Africa. If you get fed up with sunbathing, we can arrange a scuba-diving trip to see the Red Sea's sensational coral reefs.

Day 4: Mount Everest
A long day's travelling to reach Mount Everest on the border of Tibet and Nepal. At 8,848 metres, it's the highest peak on Earth and part of the Himalayas, the world's highest mountain range. For expert climbers only.

* An itinerary's a sort of list telling you where you're going and what you're going to see. Just in case you were wandering, sorry, wondering.

Day 5: Sundarbans

After a good rest, we trek through the steamy Sundarbans. This massive mangrove swamp grows around the Bay of Bengal. But mind the mudskippers. These freaky fish really can live out of water.

Day 6: Gobi Desert

Next stop, the Gobi Desert in Central Asia. In summer, temperatures sizzle at 45°C. But in winter, it's a freezing – 40°C. Some people say the Gobi's haunted but we can't guarantee you'll see a ghost.

Day 7: Yangtze River

A thrilling boat trip down the raging Yangtze River in China. At 6,376 km, it's the world's third-longest river and flows from Tibet into the East China Sea. Lifejackets will be provided in case the river floods.

Day 8: Mount Fuji

Today's highlight is a visit to Mount Fuji. At 3,776 m, it's Japan's highest peak. If you fancy climbing up, you'll be in good company. Each year, thousands of pilgrims climb Mount Fuji to see the sacred shrine at the top.

Day 9: Borneo rainforest

A day spent strolling through the bloomin' rainforest of Borneo. Plenty of time to ogle an orang-utan or stare at a stinking rafflesia flower (hold your nose). By the way, Borneo's the third-largest island in the world.

Day 10: Krakatoa

And finally, we round off our tour with a visit to Krakatoa, a tiny island between Java and Sumatra. In 1883, this vile volcano erupted with the loudest sound ever heard (see page 23). Nothing like going out with a bang.

67

Asia's enormous. In fact, it's the largest continent on Earth. It stretches from the sunny Mediterranean Sea to the Pacific Ocean, and from the icy Arctic to the equator. To get off on the right foot, here are some more awesome facts about Asia.

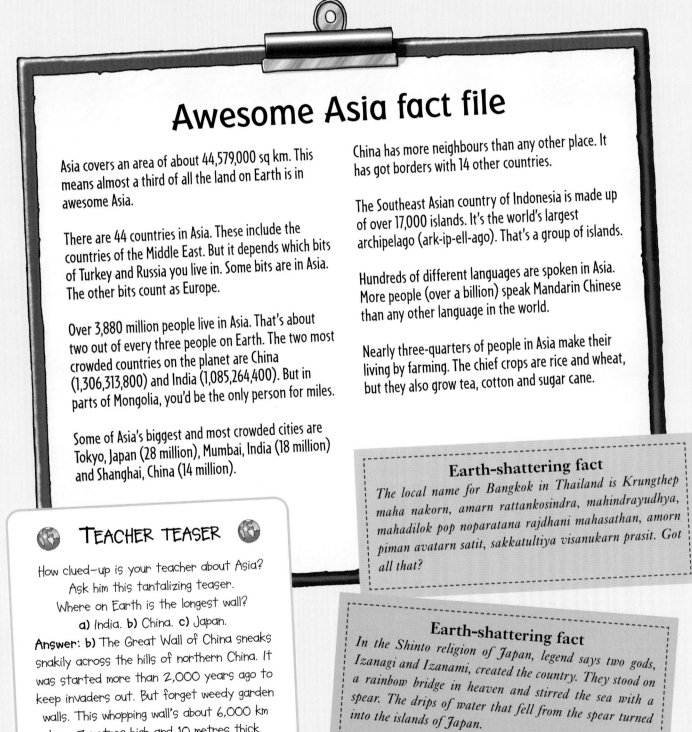

Awesome Asia fact file

Asia covers an area of about 44,579,000 sq km. This means almost a third of all the land on Earth is in awesome Asia.

There are 44 countries in Asia. These include the countries of the Middle East. But it depends which bits of Turkey and Russia you live in. Some bits are in Asia. The other bits count as Europe.

Over 3,880 million people live in Asia. That's about two out of every three people on Earth. The two most crowded countries on the planet are China (1,306,313,800) and India (1,085,264,400). But in parts of Mongolia, you'd be the only person for miles.

Some of Asia's biggest and most crowded cities are Tokyo, Japan (28 million), Mumbai, India (18 million) and Shanghai, China (14 million).

China has more neighbours than any other place. It has got borders with 14 other countries.

The Southeast Asian country of Indonesia is made up of over 17,000 islands. It's the world's largest archipelago (ark-ip-ell-ago). That's a group of islands.

Hundreds of different languages are spoken in Asia. More people (over a billion) speak Mandarin Chinese than any other language in the world.

Nearly three-quarters of people in Asia make their living by farming. The chief crops are rice and wheat, but they also grow tea, cotton and sugar cane.

TEACHER TEASER

How clued-up is your teacher about Asia?
Ask him this tantalizing teaser.
Where on Earth is the longest wall?
a) India. b) China. c) Japan.
Answer: b) The Great Wall of China sneaks snakily across the hills of northern China. It was started more than 2,000 years ago to keep invaders out. But forget weedy garden walls. This whopping wall's about 6,000 km long, 7 metres high and 10 metres thick.

Earth-shattering fact
The local name for Bangkok in Thailand is Krungthep maha nakorn, amarn rattankosindra, mahindrayudhya, mahadilok pop noparatana rajdhani mahasathan, amorn piman avatarn satit, sakkatultiya visanukarn prasit. Got all that?

Earth-shattering fact
In the Shinto religion of Japan, legend says two gods, Izanagi and Izanami, created the country. They stood on a rainbow bridge in heaven and stirred the sea with a spear. The drips of water that fell from the spear turned into the islands of Japan.

Sacred places

Did you know that awesome Asia's where the world's really big religions began? Today, followers of these faiths live all over the globe. But their most sacred cities are in Asia. In case you don't get time to visit them all, Parky's bought his postcard collection along…

Sacred city: JERUSALEM
Country: Israel
Ancient Jerusalem's a sacred city for followers of three faiths. For Jews, it's the ancient capital of the land God promised them. For Christians, it's where Jesus spent his last days on Earth. For Muslims (who follow Islam), it's where the Prophet Muhammad visited heaven. Awesome.

Sacred city: MAKKAH
Country: Saudi Arabia
The holy city of Makkah's sacred for Muslims. It's the city where the Prophet Muhammad was born in AD 570. For Muslims, Muhammad's special because Allah (God) chose him to teach people about Islam. Each year, millions of Muslims make a special journey to Makkah to worship at the sacred sites.

Sacred city: AMRITSAR
Country: India
Amazing Amritsar is a sacred place for Sikhs (who follow Sikhism). Its holiest building is the glittering Golden Temple, which stands in the middle of a lake. Sikhs from all over the world come here to worship. A copy of the Sikhs' sacred book, called the Guru Granth Sahib, is carefully kept inside the Temple.

Sacred city: VARANASI
Country: India
For Hindus (followers of Hinduism), their holiest city is Varanasi. Hindus think this is the place the great god, Shiva, chose as his home on Earth. The city lies along the banks of the River Ganges, which is sacred for Hindus. They believe it flows from heaven, and bathing in its water washes away their sins.

AMAZING AFRICA

1f Asia's given you a taste for adventure, why not check out Africa? Africa's mind-boggling. Mind-bogglingly big and exciting, that is. Wakey, wakey. There's no time for a quick snooze. There's so much to see and do, you'll need to get a move on with our Amazing African Adventure.

Day 1: Atlas Mountains
Our tour starts in the Atlas Mountains, which run across North Africa from Morocco to Tunisia. Afternoon visit to a Berber village. The Berbers are the local people who live by farming and making carpets and jewellery to sell.

Day 3: River Nile
A relaxing morning boat trip along part of the record-breaking River Nile. The Nile flows for 6,695 km and is the longest river in the world. Another of its claims to fame is that the ancient Egyptians once lived along its banks.

Day 4: Central African rainforest
Today we trek through the hot, steamy rainforest in Central Africa. It's teeming with wicked wildlife. Watch out for the rare okapi (it looks a bit like a zebra without so many stripes). It's so shy, it hasn't been seen for years.

Day 2: Sahara Desert
Next stop is the sensational Sahara Desert. It covers a third of Africa and is the world's largest desert. Check out the ancient rock paintings and the tallest sand dunes on Earth. Camel ride (optional).

Day 5: Lake Victoria
A delightful day at Lake Victoria, Africa's largest lake. It lies right on the equator between Kenya, Uganda and Tanzania. It covers 69,484 sq km and is 82 metres deep at its deepest point. Fishing trips on this monster lake can be arranged.

Day 6: Mount Kilimanjaro

After an early breakfast, we head up Mount Kilimanjaro in Tanzania. At 5,896 m, it's Africa's highest peak. Sturdy boots and warm clothes essential. Even though it's on the equator, the peak's permanently covered in snow.

Day 7: Great Rift Valley

Next stop, the Great Rift Valley, a vast crack in the Earth's crust about 8,700 km long. It was formed when violent volcanic eruptions caused huge blocks of land to sink. It has got spectacular scenery and luscious lakes. Fancy a dip, anyone?

Day 8: Victoria Falls

A flying visit to the Victoria Falls where the mighty River Zambezi plunges over a 108-metre-high cliff.

Day 9: Okavango Delta

We journey south to the awesome Okavango Delta. Most rivers flow into the sea but not the odd Okavango. It sinks into the Kalahari Desert instead. But in the rainy season, the river floods and the desert delta becomes a maze of steamy swamps and lagoons. Perfect for a hippo hang-out.

Day 10: Kalahari Desert

And speaking of the Kalahari Desert ... this is where we end our tour. If you're feeling energetic, you might like to stay on and go hunting with the local San people. Anyone speak fluent Click?*

* The languages spoken by the San people are made up of clicking sounds. And they take years and years to learn. One false click and you can change a word's meaning completely.

Africa's the second-largest continent, after awesome Asia. Why not astonish your good old geography teacher with some more amazing Africa facts?

Amazing Africa fact file

Africa covers an area of about 30,065,000 sq km. That's about a fifth of the Earth's surface.

The continent's 8,000 km from north to south, and about 7,500 km from east to west. So you'd better start walking.

There are 53 countries in Africa, the most on any continent. Don't believe me. Go on, count them up.

Africa has 30,539 km of crooked coast.

The biggest countries are Sudan (2,500,000 sq km) and Algeria (2,381,741 sq km).

Madagascar's an island off the south-east coast. At a massive 587,041 sq km, it's the fourth-biggest island in the world.

Over 800 million people live in Africa. That's about a tenth of all the people on Earth.

The largest African cities are Lagos, Nigeria (13.5 million), Cairo, Egypt (11 million) and Kinshasa, Congo (5.5 million).

The highest temperature ever recorded was 58°C in Al'Aziziyah, Libya in 1922. And that was in the shade!

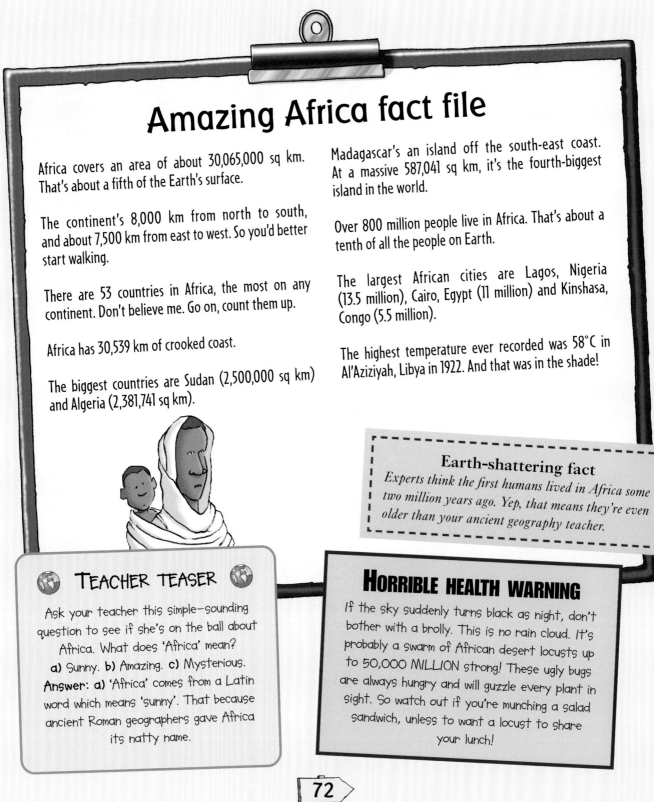

Earth-shattering fact
Experts think the first humans lived in Africa some two million years ago. Yep, that means they're even older than your ancient geography teacher.

TEACHER TEASER

Ask your teacher this simple-sounding question to see if she's on the ball about Africa. What does 'Africa' mean?
a) Sunny. b) Amazing. c) Mysterious.
Answer: a) 'Africa' comes from a Latin word which means 'sunny'. That because ancient Roman geographers gave Africa its natty name.

HORRIBLE HEALTH WARNING

If the sky suddenly turns black as night, don't bother with a brolly. This is no rain cloud. It's probably a swarm of African desert locusts up to 50,000 MILLION strong! These ugly bugs are always hungry and will guzzle every plant in sight. So watch out if you're munching a salad sandwich, unless to want a locust to share your lunch!

Wicked wildlife

One thing Africa's world famous for is its wicked wildlife. So keep your eyes peeled, won't you? To show you what to look out for, here's some snaps Parky took on an earlier trip. But be careful. Get too close to these beauties, and they might just snap back. And talking of snaps…

Name: HIPPOPOTAMUS
Where found: Rivers, lakes and swamps.
Appearance: Big, barrel-shaped body. Short, stumpy legs.
Horrible habit: Fighting.
They might look cute and cuddly but watch out for a hippo in a huff. Giant gnashers up to 50 cm long grow in their bottom jaws. These are used as lethal weapons and can cause wicked wounds, and even death.

Name: OSTRICH
Where found: Grasslands.
Appearance: A gigantic, and I mean gigantic, bird. Very long, very spindly legs.
Horrible habit: Kicking.
Ostriches are the biggest birds in the world. And they're much too bloomin' big to fly. But they use their long legs for running faster than a horse. Oh, and for giving their enemies a good kick!

Name: NILE CROCODILE
Where found: River mouths.
Appearance: Long, scaly bodies. Long snouts. Razor-sharp teeth.
Horrible habit: Eating people.
And rhinos, wildebeest, giraffes and lions… Once this fella gets his chops around you, there's no escape. One croc killed in Botswana had a whole human body, two goats and half a donkey in its stomach.

Name: GABOON VIPER
Where found: Tropical rainforests.
Appearance: Cunning camouflage to match the dead leaves on the forest floor where it lives.
Horrible habit: Biting.
This vile viper's got the longest poisonous fangs of any snake. And it'll sink them into your flesh if you pester it. Trouble is, you might not see it until it's too late. So you won't know you've put your foot in it.

ENORMOUS NORTH AMERICA

Our next stop's the enormous continent of North America. Anyone been there before? Don't worry, you won't have time to feel tired. We've put together a top-notch North American tour that'll keep you on your toes. So best foot forward or you'll be late for the first stop on our Enormous North American Adventure.

Day 1: Hawaii

Our tour starts in Hawaii, 4,000 km off the south-west coast of the USA, in the Pacific Ocean. Perfect for a relaxing holiday. Some of the beaches have black sand, but don't let that put you off! The sand's made from crushed-up bits of volcanic rock. Sorry, I forgot to mention these idyllic islands are actually the tops of hot-tempered volcanoes. But they erupt very gently so you're quite safe to sunbathe.

Day 2: Denali

A change of scenery and climate next, with a visit to Denali in chilly Alaska. At 6,194 metres high, it's North America's highest mountain. In fact, it got its name from a Native American word meaning 'high one'. It's also called Mount McKinley, after a US president.

Day 3: Rocky Mountains

Heading south, we reach the mighty Rocky mountains, which run for 4,800 km down the continent from Alaska to New Mexico. If you're feeling energetic, you can take your pick from climbing, hiking or canoeing down some of the rivers that start flowing in the raging Rockies.

Day 4: The prairies

Today we have a long, dusty drive through the vast open plains of the prairies right in the middle of the USA. These used to be rolling grasslands where millions of buffalo grazed. Sadly, they're long gone now and the prairies have been turned into monster wheat fields.

Day 5: Niagara Falls

Next stop, a thrilling trip to Niagara Falls on the border between Canada and the USA. You can gawp at these world-famous waterfalls from Goat Island. But prepare for a soaking. Or, if you really want to make a splash, take the elevator to the Cave of the Winds. It's tucked away behind the falling water.

Day 6: Great Lakes

A short hop to visit the five Great Lakes. The Niagara Falls flow between Lakes Erie and Ontario, so you've already notched up two of them. The others are Superior, Michigan and Huron. Whopping Lake Superior's the largest freshwater lake on Earth.

Day 7: Mammoth Caves

A whole day spent underground in the massive Mammoth Caves, Kentucky, USA. It's the world's longest cave network, with over 560 km of caves and passages already mapped and hundreds more left to explore. Some caves have brilliant names like Giant's Coffin and Bottomless Pit. Torches will be provided in case you fall in.

Day 8: Mississippi River

Heading south again, we make for the mighty Mississippi River. It's 3,780 km long but joins up with the Missouri River to form the third-largest river system in the world. Its nicknames include Big Muddy and Old Man River. Now, please be careful getting into the boat.

Day 9: Gulf of Mexico

An overnight boat trip down the Mississippi south to its delta (see page 37 for more about how deltas form) in the Gulf of Mexico. The Gulf's horribly rich in precious oil and you won't be able to miss the thousands of oil rigs built to pump out the oil.

Day 10: Sonoran Desert

We spend our last day in the bone-dry Sonoran Desert, which stretches across the border between the USA and Mexico. Keep your cameras handy. There's plenty to snap. It's home to some fabulous wildlife, including giant saguaro cacti, mountain lions, and, er, rattlesnakes. Help!

After Asia and Africa, North America's the third-biggest continent. No wonder you're tired after your tour. So while you're taking a well-earned rest, here are some big, brash facts.

Enormous North America fact file

North America covers an area of 24,256,000 sq km – that's about a sixth of the Earth's surface.

It's home to more than 500 million people.

There are 23 countries in North America, including Canada, the USA, Mexico, the countries of Central America and the world's biggest island, Greenland.

By far, the biggest countries are Canada (9,976,169 sq km) and the USA (9,363,123 sq km). In fact, Canada's the second-largest country in the world, with the USA close behind in fourth place.

The most popular sports played in sports-mad North America are baseball, basketball, ice hockey, American football and soccer (in Central America).

North America's famous for its big, bustling cities. Check out the biggest cities in the USA – New York (16 million people), Los Angeles (13 million people) and Chicago (7 million people).

The enormous USA is the world's richest and most powerful country. Its leading products include iron and steel, timber, cars and electronic equipment.

HORRIBLE HEALTH WARNING

Mind you don't catch Rocky Mountain spotted fever, which is spread by rats and ticks. Symptoms include a raging fever, followed by shivering, then you'll break out in bright pink spots. Oh, and you'll die if you don't get to a doctor fast.

TEACHER TEASER

Before your teacher nips out for her tea-break, catch her out with this quick-fire question. Who or what was America named after?
a) A Native American chief. **b)** A type of pizza. **c)** An Italian explorer.
Answer: c) America was named after Italian explorer (and pickle-seller), Amerigo Vespucci (1454–1512). But he got the honour by accident when a gormless geographer wrote his name on a map by mistake. In fact, Amerigo never quite made it to North America, though he did sail along the South American coast.

Earth-shattering fact
Until the sixteenth century, the local people of North America were Native Americans. Then settlers from Europe began to arrive and take over their lands. Today, there are very few Native Americans left. In the USA, many of them live on land given back by the government. They are working hard to keep their customs alive.

Really big buildings

If you fancy living the high life, North America's the perfect place to start. It's famous for its towering skyscrapers, which are among the highest buildings in the world. But you'll need to have a good head for heights. Some of these beauties are horribly tall.

Name: EMPIRE STATE BUILDING
City: New York, USA
Height: 381 metres
Completed: 1931
Towering facts:
• It has 102 storeys, reached by 62 elevators (or 1,800 steps).
• It took just 410 days to build, at a rate of 4.5 storeys a week.
• The mast on the top was designed for mooring giant passenger airships. But it was only used twice.

Name: CN TOWER
City: Toronto, Canada
Height: 555 metres to tip of mast
Completed: 1975
Towering facts:
• It's the world's tallest structure but doesn't strictly count as a building. It's used for TV transmission.
• Two-thirds up is the Skypod, which has viewing rooms, a nightclub and a revolving restaurant.
• It's struck by lightning about 200 times a year.

Name: SEARS TOWER
City: Chicago, USA
Height: 443 metres
Completed: 1973
Towering facts:
• It's the tallest building in North America with 110 storeys. In strong winds, the top floor sways a metre from side to side.
• The total floor space inside the building is the same as 65 soccer pitches.
• Six special robots automatically brush, rinse and dry the Tower's hundreds of windows so you don't need to call a window cleaner.

Name: CHRYSLER BUILDING
City: New York, USA
Height: 319 metres
Completed: 1930
Towering facts:
• It won the 'Race to the Sky' competition to become the world's tallest skyscraper. But four months later, it was beaten by the Empire State Building.
• It's built in a striking style called Art Deco with shining steel and glass arches.
• The outside's decorated with symbols like eagles, which appeared on the bonnets of Chrysler cars.

SENSATIONAL SOUTH AMERICA

Next stop, South America – a sightseer's paradise. From rolling grasslands and snow-capped mountains, to lush rainforests and bone-dry deserts, South America has got some of the most spectacular scenery on the planet. You'll see it all on our Sensational South America Adventure.

Day 1: Galapagos Islands

Our tour starts on the gorgeous Galapagos Islands, about 1,000 km west of Ecuador. They're famous for their wildlife, which is found nowhere else on Earth. So get ready to gawp at giant tortoises and marvel at lizards that live on seaweed.

Day 2: Angel Falls

Back to the mainland today and a thrilling trip to Angel Falls in Venezuela. Here the River Churun plunges 979 metres down the side of Devil's Mountain, making a splash as the world's highest waterfall. The Falls get their angelic name from American pilot Jimmy Angel, who spotted them in 1935.

Day 3: River Amazon

A full day spent canoeing down the River Amazon. At an awesome 6,400 km long, it's the world second–longest river. It has got more water flowing in it than any other river on Earth. So mind you don't fall in. By the way, the world's biggest rainforest grows along the river's banks.

Day 4: Andes Mountains

Next stop, we board a plane for a flight over the Andes, the world's longest mountain range. These freaky peaks stretch for a staggering 7,250 km right down the west coast of South America. There'll be time for a short walk after lunch, but many of these massive mountains are over 6,000 metres tall so we won't be able to climb them all.

Day 5: Lake Titicaca

While we're exploring the Andes, we drop in to Lake Titicaca on the border of Bolivia and Peru. It's 3,812 metres above sea level, making it the highest navigable* lake on Earth. Our day includes a visit to a Uru village. The Uru are the local lake people who live on floating reed islands in the lake.

Day 6: Atacama Desert

We head south to the Atacama Desert, wedged between the Andes and the Pacific Ocean along the west coast of Chile. This desperate desert might lie next to the ocean but it's officially the driest place on Earth. Some parts had no rain at all for hundreds of years. So make sure you fill up your water bottle before you leave the bus.

Day 7: Easter Island

A long day's sail to isolated Easter Island, 3,700 km off the west coast of Chile in the South Pacific Ocean. It's famous for its huge stone statues, which were carved hundreds of years ago. The island was named by European sailors who spotted it on Easter Day 1722.

Day 8: Aconcagua

Next, we trek to Aconcagua in Argentina. At 6,962 tall, this extinct (that means long-dead) volcano is the highest peak in the whole Andes. The first person to climb Aconcagua was plucky Swiss climber Matthias Zurbriggen in 1897. He battled gale-force winds, blizzards and frostbite to reach the top in 1897. Fancy following in his footsteps?

Day 9: Pampas

A scenic drive across the gorgeous grasslands that cover the middle of Argentina. These rolling plains are called the pampas and they're used for growing grain and beans, and grazing cattle. Why not spend the afternoon with a real-life gaucho (cowboy), helping him herd cattle on a ranch?

Day 10: Tierra del Fuego

The last leg of our tour takes us right down to the southernmost tip of South America and the islands of Tierra del Fuego. Their name means 'Land of Fire' but they're actually wet and windswept, with lots of massive glaciers flowing down from the mountains.

*Navigable is just the posh way of saying the lake's large and calm enough for you to sail a boat on.

I told you South America was sensational – and you've only scratched the surface. While you're getting your breath back, check out some more sensational facts.

Sensational South America fact file

South America covers an area of 17,819,000 sq km, making it the world's fourth-largest continent.

Over 350 million people live in South America. That's about six per cent of the planet's population.

There are 12 countries in South America. Brazil's the biggest (8,456,510 sq km) and the fifth largest in the world. Argentina's in second place (2,777, 815 sq km).

About three-quarters of South America lies south of the equator. It's just 970 km from Cape Horn, at the southernmost tip, to ice-bound Antarctica.

South America's almost entirely surrounded by sea. The Caribbean Sea lies to the north, the Atlantic Ocean to the east and the vast Pacific to the west.

The only land border is a narrow strip in the north called the Isthmus of Panama. It links Central America to South America.

Spanish is the main language spoken in South America. Portuguese is spoken in Brazil. That's because for centuries, South America was ruled by Spain and Portugal.

Fancy a nice cup of coffee? The coffee beans probably came from Brazil, which grows about four million tonnes of coffee a year. It also grows loads of sugar cane, cotton and bananas.

 TEACHER TEASER

Put your teacher on the spot with this question about city living. Which is the biggest city in South America?
a) São Paulo, Brazil. **b)** Buenos Aires, Argentina. **c)** Rio de Janeiro, Brazil.
Answer: a) About 17.5 million people in São Paulo, making it the biggest city in South America and one of the most crowded cities in the world.

HORRIBLE HEALTH WARNING

If you're thinking of scaling an Andean peak, try picking one that's not actually erupting. In 1879, British climber Edward Whymper set out to climb Cotopaxi, a violent volcano. Incredibly, he made it to the top despite getting ash up his nose (and in his eyes and ears) and pitching his tent on roasting-hot lava. Read more about adventurous Ed on page 21.

Earth-shattering fact
Tortoises living on the Galapagos Islands can grow up to 1.5 metres long and weigh a quarter of a tonne. What's more, these record-breaking reptiles can live for up to 200 years. No, I'm not telling whoppers. Astonishingly, it's all true.

Whopping wildlife

If it's whopping wildlife you're after, you've come to the right place. Some sensational animals live in South America and they've all got one thing in common. Anyone guess what it is? Nope, they don't all smell terrible. Give up? They're all WHOPPING, that's what. Time to hop on our safari bus.

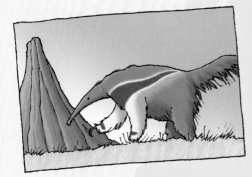

Name: GIANT ANTEATER
Habitat: South American pampas
Vital statistics: This giant's body's over 1 metre long with another metre of bushy tail. And its appetite's enormous to match. It eats an awesome 20,000 ants a day, which it laps up with its 60-cm-long tongue. That's like having a tongue as long as your arm! Think how useful that would be for slurping ice cream.

Name: CAPYBARA
Habitat: South America lakes, rivers and marshes
Vital statistics: This remarkable rodent looks a bit like a guinea pig and in fact they're closely related. But forget your sweet, furry pet at home. This whopper stands 60 cm tall and is the size of a proper pig. It spends the day lazing about by a lake, occasionally waddling into the water to graze on bits of veg.

Name: ANACONDA
Habitat: Amazon and Orinoco Rivers
Vital statistics: This sensational slitherer is the world's biggest snake. It's 10 metres long and a metre around the middle. Its uses its massive body to squeeze its favourite snacks of small deer and monkeys to death. Don't panic – you won't end up as lunch. Even an awesome anaconda would find it awkward to gobble down a whole human.

Name: ANDEAN CONDOR
Habitat: Andes mountains
Vital statistics: The condor's a monster bird with a monster wingspan to match. From tip to tip, its wings measure a massive 3 metres across. It uses its whopping wings to soar high about the mountain slopes, on the look-out for dead animals to eat. It can eat two-thirds of its weight in one sitting, then goes without food for weeks. Burp!

EXTRAORDINARY EUROPE

Our next continent is Europe, and what an extraordinary place it is. From the frozen north to the warm, sunny south, you're sure to find something to write home about. Our Extraordinary European Adventure's about to begin so you'd better hop on board.

Day 1: Iceland

Our tour starts in icy Iceland, so everyone except Parky will need to wrap up warm. This incredible island lies on the Mid-Atlantic Ridge, where the Earth's splitting apart. So you'll get to see erupting volcanoes, and we'll throw in a few groovy glaciers for good measure.

Day 2: Norwegian fjords

The jagged west coast of Norway's a must for serious sightseers. Freaky fjords (fee-yords) are valleys gouged out by glaciers, which later filled with sea. Boats trips can be arranged.

Day 3: Lough Neagh

Heading south, we reach Northern Ireland and the boggy shores of Lough Neagh. It covers 400 sq km and is the biggest lake in the British Isles. But forget geography. Legend says the lake was made by a giant, Finn MacCool, when he scooped up a huge boulder and chucked it into the sea.

Day 4: Baltic Sea

A day spent by the Baltic Sea. It's part of the Atlantic Ocean and one of the busiest seas in the world. Until a few years ago, the Baltic wasn't a pretty sight. But don't worry. People have been working very hard to clean up the sea and stop ships spilling oil, which kills off wildlife.

Day 5: Alps

A change of scenery today as we visit the awesome Alps. These freaky peaks run for 1,200 km from France, through Switzerland and Italy, and into Austria. If you're feeling energetic, why not try climbing Mont Blanc. At 4,807 metres tall, it's the highest mountain in the Alps so you'll get a brilliant view from the top.

Day 6: River Danube

From the Alps, it's a short-ish hop to the Danube, Europe's second-longest river. It flows for about 2,850 km from its source in Germany to its delta in the Black Sea. The delta's home to hundreds of different kinds of birds so have your binoculars handy.

Day 7: Mount Vesuvius

Today could go with a bang. We visit hot-tempered Mount Vesuvius, an active* volcano near Naples in Italy. Its earliest recorded eruption was in AD 79 when it buried the nearby town of Pompeii in ash. It last flipped its lid in 1944 so it could go up at any time.

Day 8: Mediterranean Sea

After all the excitement, we spend a relaxing day sunbathing on the shores of the Mediterranean Sea. Its warm, dry weather and long, sandy beaches make it a favourite spot for holidays. If you're going swimming, watch out for smelly sewage – the water's not as crystal clear as it should be.

Day 9: River Volga

Next stop, the raging River Volga in Russia. The vulgar Volga's the longest river in Europe, flowing for 3,530 km from its source in the hills near Moscow into the Caspian Sea. The Volga's vitally important. Hundreds of ships use it every day to carry goods between factories on the river banks.

Day 10: Mount Elbrus

Our European tour ends on a high point as we reach Mount Elbrus. It's part of the Caucasus Mountains right on the border between Europe and Asia. It's the highest mountain on the continent, standing 5,642 metres tall. But if you're feeling weary, why not take the cable car nearly to the top?

*Active means this explosive peak's still likely to blow its top at any time. Trouble is, no one knows exactly when.

By size, Europe's the second-smallest continent but it gets pretty crowded because the third-highest number of people live there. Ready to find out some more extraordinary facts about Europe?

Extraordinary Europe fact file

Europe covers an area of 10,459,000 sq km. That's about a fifteenth of the land on Earth. It's smaller than every other continent, except Australasia.

Europe stretches from the Arctic Ocean in the north to the Mediterranean in the south, and from the Atlantic Ocean in the west to the Ural Mountains in the east.

About 750 million people live in Europe - about a ninth of the world's population. Only Asia and Africa have more people living there.

Europe has 47 countries. These include Russia, the world's largest country (17 million sq km), and the Vatican City, the world's smallest (0.44 sq km).

About 50 languages are spoken in Europe and hundreds of dialects (local languages). So Hola, God morgen and Bonjour - that's 'Hello' in Spanish, Danish and French.

Europe's jagged coastline measures over 60,000 km. Straightened out, it would reach one and a half times around the Equator.

Over half of the land in Europe is used for farming and it's some of the richest farmland in the world. Farmers grow loads of wheat, barley and potatoes, and keep cattle for meat and milk.

The most practised religion in Europe is Christianity and most Christians are Roman Catholics. There are also millions of Jews and Muslims.

Earth-shattering fact

Fancy nipping between England and France but feeling seriously seasick? Why not travel under the sea instead? The Channel Tunnel opened in 1994 but it was first thought of 200 years ago. The plan was to build a candle-lit tunnel with horse-drawn carriages. Luckily, today you can catch the train.

TEACHER TEASER

Get your teacher's battered brain-cells whirring with this carefully coined question. Many countries in Europe share the same currency. What is it called?
a) Dollar. b) Peseta. c) Euro.
Answer: c) 13 countries in Europe (Greece, Germany, Holland, France, Italy, Portugal, Spain, Belgium, Luxembourg, Finland, Austria, Ireland and Slovenia) use a currency called the Euro (1 Euro = 100 cents).

Mind-boggling buildings

This tour's not just about rivers, mountains … and tunnels. It's about the people who live around the world, too. Some of these people lived hundreds of years ago so we can't drop in for a chat. But they left some mind-boggling buildings behind for us to explore. Parky's postcards will tell us all we need to know.

Name: TOWER OF LONDON
Location: London, England
The Tower's a famous ancient fortress in London. It was begun by William the Conqueror in the eleventh century so it's pretty bloomin' old. The Tower was a royal palace but it was also a place to keep prisoners before they got their heads chopped off. Big, black birds called ravens flap around the Tower and legend says if the ravens ever fly away, England will fall!

Name: PALACE OF KNOSSOS
Location: Crete, Greece
The glittering palace of Knossos was the luxurious headquarters of the mighty Minoans, who ruled Crete 4,000 years ago. But they weren't alone. Legend says a hideous half-man, half-bull called a minotaur lurked in maze in the palace as well. This monstrous minotaur had terrible table manners. He liked to chomp on little boys and girls to keep his strength up. Nice.

Name: ST BASIL'S CATHEDRAL
Location: Moscow, Russia
You won't be able to miss St Basil's Cathedral. Head for Red Square and look for a barmy building topped by brightly-coloured … onions. No, not real onions, they're actually domes but they look like, oh never mind. The cathedral was built in the sixteenth century by Ivan the Terrible to celebrate a great battle victory. Ivan really lived up to his name. He had the architect blinded so he could never design anything as beautiful as St Basil's again.

Name: ALHAMBRA PALACE
Location: Granada, Spain
The Alhambra's a dazzling city of fairy-tale palaces and courtyards built in the fourteenth century by the Muslim rulers of southern Spain. It was so beautiful they thought they'd created a piece of paradise on Earth. Check out the exquisite Court of the Lions with its life-like marble lions or chill out in the gorgeous gardens nearby. After a long day, it's a heavenly place to hang out.

ASTONISHING AUSTRALASIA

Our final far-out continent is Australasia on the other side of the world. And what an astonishing place it is. There's so much to see, so let's get straight on with our Astonishing Australasian Adventure. And now that Wanda's had a bit of a breather, she's ready to hit the road again.

Day 1: Papua New Guinea rainforest

We spend our first day in the rainforest of Papua New Guinea. Keep your eyes peeled and you might see a brilliant bird of paradise with its dazzling feathers. It might be your last chance. So many trees are being chopped down for their valuable timber, the rainforest's under serious threat.

Day 2: Mount Wilhelm

We stay in Papua New Guinea for the next stop on our tour – lofty Mount Wilhelm. At 4,509 metres tall, it's the highest peak in the whole of Australasia. If you're feeling fit, a trek to the summit can be arranged. Or you can fly there and back by helicopter.

Day 3: Great Barrier Reef

A relaxing day spent at the Great Barrier Reef off the north-east coast of Australia. Some of you have visited the reef before (see page 35) but it's well worth another look. After all, it's the biggest coral reef on Earth and you don't get much more picturesque than that. This time, why not hop on a mini-sub for a thrilling underwater tour of the reef?

Day 4: Lake Eyre

Our next stop's enormous Lake Eyre. It measures a massive 9,300 sq. km and is the biggest lake in Australia. But don't bother putting your bathers on. This loathsome lake lies in the middle of the desert and any water quickly evaporates (turns to water vapour) in the sun. So it's usually as dry as a bone.

Day 5: Uluru

A short hop west to Uluru (it used to be called Ayers Rock). In the local Aboriginal language, its name means 'great pebble' but this isn't the sort of pebble you'd pick up on a beach. It's a massive block of sandstone in the desert, 380 metres tall. It's a sacred place for the Aborigines so please treat it with respect.

Day 6: The Outback

We stay in the desert today so have your water bottles handy. Actually, two-thirds of Australia counts as desert so you can't really miss it. Together, it's called the Outback and it's one of the hottest and driest places on Earth.

Day 7: Tasmania

Down south for a boat trip to Tasmania, 240 km off the Australian coast. Today the island's famous for its wool and fruit but it used to be used as a prison. In the nineteenth century, thousands of criminals were sent there from Britain to serve their sentences. With all that sea around them, escape was impossible.

Day 8: Mount Cook

Leaving Australia behind, we head for New Zealand and mighty Mount Cook on South Island. It's called Aoraki in the local language, which means 'cloud piercer' and this freaky peak's almost always got its head in the clouds. It's 3,754 metres high and if you don't fancy climbing it, you could go skiing instead.

Day 9: Rotorua

Journey north to Rotorua on North Island for a day of thrills and spills. Here hot volcanic rocks heat up water underground. Watch out for gushing geysers and plopping pools of boiling mud. But take a peg for your nose. The place pongs of rotten eggs (thanks to smelly gases seeping from the ground).

Day 10: Fiji

And finally, a chance for a well-earned rest on the idyllic islands of Fiji. They're some of thousands of tropical islands dotted around the Pacific Ocean. Many of them are made from coral. Others are the tips of underwater volcanoes. Enjoy your stay.

Australasia's the smallest of the continents so it's a wonder it manages to pack so much in. Stun your friends and amaze your teacher with some more astonishing Australasian facts.

Astonishing Australasia fact file

Australasia covers an area of 7,687,000 sq km - that's just 5 per cent of the Earth's land surface. Almost all of it's made up of Australia, which measures a whopping 7,617,930 sq km, almost as big as the USA.

Apart from Australia, the continent includes ten other countries, such as New Zealand, Papua New Guinea and tiny islands scattered about the Pacific Ocean.

Australia looks like an island and it's surrounded by sea. But geographers count is as a continent in its own right because it's so bloomin' big. In fact, it's the only the country that's also a continent.

If you count Australia as a continent, New Guinea's the world's second-largest island (after Greenland). Put together, the two halves of the island cover about 785,753 sq km. Horribly confusing, isn't it?

Only about 33 million people live in Australasia. That's fewer than in any other continent apart from Antarctica. About 20 million of them live in Australia, mostly in cities around the south-east coast.

The earliest Australians were the Aboriginals. They've lived there for over 40,000 years. The arrival of European settlers threatened to destroy their traditional lifestyle. Today, they are fighting to win their lands back.

About a quarter of all the world's wool comes from Australia. Sheep are kept on huge farms in the outback called stations. But you'd be waiting a long time for a train. These farms are so isolated, the only way to reach them is by plane.

The oldest rocks ever found on Earth come from the Jack Hills near Perth, Australia. Geographers reckon they're an ancient 4,300 million years old (the rocks, not the geographers).

Earth-shattering fact

So you've checked out Africa, Asia, South America, North America, Australasia and Europe. But hang on, that only adds up to six continents and they are actually seven in all. Can you guess what the missing continent is? Give up? It's icy Antarctica, at the southern end of the Earth. Antarctica's the fifth-largest continent by size but the only continent where no horrible humans live permanently.

TEACHER TEASER

Dig deep into your teacher's down-under know-how with this question. What is the capital of Australia?
a) Canberra. **b)** Sydney. **c)** Melbourne.
Answer: a) Sydney's certainly bigger and more famous (check out its stunning Opera House) so many people think it's the capital but that's actually Canberra. Did your teacher get caught out?

Weird wildlife

Because Australasia's so isolated, many of its astonishing animals are found nowhere else in the world. And you can thank your lucky stars because some of these beauties are among the deadliest creatures on Earth. Here are just a few of them and some reasons to avoid them at all costs. Don't worry, you won't have to get too close.

Name: FUNNEL-WEB SPIDER
Where found: Forests, gardens and garden sheds.
Appearance: About 5 cm long with glossy, dark brown body and hairy legs.
Reasons to avoid: This sneaky spider's poisonous bite could kill you in an hour or two. First you'd get aches and pains and start sweating. Then you'd turn blue and froth at the mouth. Unless you could get to a doctor fast, you'd soon be a gonner.

Name: FIERCE SNAKE
Where found: Rivers and creeks.
Appearance: Yellowish body about 1.7 metres long with a black head and beady black eyes.
Reasons to avoid: The good news is the frightful fierce snake normally only poisons plague rats. Besides, it's so shy and secretive, it hardly even comes across horrible humans. The bad news is it's the most poisonous land snake and if this beauty bit you, you wouldn't stand a chance. And it's not alone. Nine out of ten of the world's deadliest snakes live in ... Australia. Very nasty.

Name: CONE SHELL
Where found: Coral reefs.
Appearance: A sea snail with a speckly, er, cone-shaped shell
Reasons to avoid: Cone shells might look pretty but pick one up at your peril. You could get a deadly dose of poison from a harpoon-like tooth under its shell. You'll feel woefully weak and wobbly, and start slurring your words. Soon you won't be able to breathe or move. Unfortunately, there's no cure yet, so in a few hours, you'll be dead. Sorry.

Name: SEA WASP
Where found: Calm waters near the coast.
Appearance: Pale blue and see-through with a box-shaped body and 3-metre long tentacles.
Reasons to avoid: This small but deadly jellyfish is the most dangerous creature IN THE SEA. Its terrible trailing tentacles shoot out enough poison to kill 60 people. The pain's so agonizing that you'll probably go into shock and drown before you even reach the shore. If you've got some vinegar handy, dab it on the wound. This stops the tentacles stinging. You hope.

ANCIENT CITIES GUIDE

Today, city living's all the rage but, until about 8,000 years ago, cities hadn't even been heard of. Then people started to settle down, instead of pottering around from place to place. They built villages, which grew into towns, which grew into cities. You get the picture. Fancy a quick city break? Why not check out this special city edition of our Horrible Holiday Guide? Ready to take a trip back in time?

BABYLON, modern-day Iraq
Potted history: Babylon was built on the banks of the River Euphrates, which was dead handy for transport and water supplies. The magnificent capital of Mesopotamia, Babylon was fabulously wealthy and packed with gorgeous palaces and temples. Enter the city through the great Ishtar Gate. Look out for the dragon and bull decorations on its dazzling bright blue tiles.
Don't miss: The Hanging Gardens. Terrace-loads of exotic trees and flowers planted by green-fingered King Nebuchadnezzar. One of the Seven Wonders of the Ancient World.

ATHENS, Greece
Potted history: The largest city in ancient Greece with over 250,000 people. Awesome Athens was built on two levels – a rocky hill called the Acropolis and the rest of the city around the bottom. The Acropolis was a sacred place with top-notch temples and shrines to the gods. Handily, the city also had its own nearby port (Piraeus) on the coast, which helped it grow filthy rich through trade.
Don't miss: The Parthenon. Head to the Acropolis to see this temple to the goddess, Athene. The city's named after her. This temple was built of brilliant white marble in the fifth century BC.

ANCIENT ROME, Italy

Potted history: The headquarters of the mighty Roman Empire, Rome was built on seven hills overlooking the raging River Tiber. There are masses of mind-boggling buildings to see, built by the Roman emperors to show off their wealth and power. To find out what's going on in the city, head for the Forum. It's a marketplace in the city centre where you can hear all the latest gossip.

Don't miss: The Colosseum. Get your entrance ticket here. But hurry, it's a horribly popular place to hang out.

STAR ATTRACTION!

The colossal Colosseum in Rome was the place to watch gory gladiator fights and bloodthirsty Romans were potty about them. The Colosseum had space for 50,000 spectators but it paid to book early because people packed in like sardines. Choose a seat not too close to the action so you don't get horribly blood-splattered.

GREAT ZIMBABWE, Zimbabwe

Potted history: This great, stone-walled city dates back to the thirteenth century. Geographers think it was the capital of a great empire that grew rich on trading in gold and ivory. But any gold's long gone. No one knows for certain who built the city or lived there. It may once have had as many as 40,000 inhabitants but they seem to have disappeared without a trace. Spooky.

Don't miss: The Great Enclosure. It's not the enclosure itself but the walls around it that are worth a look. They're a whopping 5 metres thick and 10 metres high, and the stones fit so tightly together that they don't need any cement.

> **Earth-shattering fact**
> *Where on Earth was the world's first-ever city? Geographers reckon it might have been Catal Huyuk in Turkey, which was built about 9,000 years ago.*

Many of these sights are no longer standing or have been reduced to a worn-out old ruin. Bet your geography teacher knows just how that feels.

91

MODERN CITIES GUIDE

With so many cities to visit, it's impossible to cram them all in. So in the second part of our city guide, we concentrate on bringing you bang up-to-date with the low-down on the latest cities to be seen in. But there's no time for dawdling. Yes, I know your feet are killing you but we're almost on the last leg of our tour.

LONDON

Potted history: London's the capital city of England. It's built along the banks of the River Thames, and for centuries was a world-famous port. There are so many sensational sights to see, it's tricky to know where to start. You could jump on a boat and head down the river. Keep your eyes peeled for the historical Houses of Parliament, Shakespeare's Globe Theatre and London Bridge.

Don't miss: Buckingham Palace. It's Queen Elizabeth II's official London home and its 600 rooms are packed with priceless paintings and treasures. The Royal Standard flag flies when the Queen's at home.

PARIS

Potted history: The fabulous capital city of France, Paris began as a fishing village but quickly became an important Roman town. Today, it's packed with famous streets and fashionable shops. Not to mention local landmarks like Notre Dame Cathedral, the Louvre, the Arc de Triomphe and the Pompidou Centre. An old song says spring's the best time to go to Paris, but we recommend a visit at anytime.

Don't miss: The Eiffel Tower. Hope you've got a good head for heights.

STAR ATTRACTION!

The elegant Eiffel Tower in Paris was built by top engineer Gustave Eiffel, in 1889. It's 300 metres tall and made from over 7,000 tonnes of top-notch iron. In the 1920s, a cunning con man tried to sell the tower for scrap. Luckily, his potty plan backfired and the tower's still standing. If you can't face the stairs, why not take the lift right to the top for a lovely view.

MOSCOW

Potted history: The capital city of Russia, Moscow used to be mostly built of wood so no wonder it kept burning down. If that wasn't bad enough, Tsar (king) Peter the Great moved the capital to St Petersburg (which he named after himself) in 1703 but it was shifted back 200 years later. Today, you can take a stroll around Red Square or pay a visit to the Bolshoi Ballet. Spring and summer are the best times to go. In winter, temperatures can plummet to a fr-fr-freezing -25°C.

Don't miss: The Kremlin. This formidable fortress overlooks Red Square. Inside are palaces, cathedrals and the headquarters of the government. A great bell tower is said to mark the exact centre of Moscow.

BEIJING

Potted history: It's China's second-biggest city (next to Shanghai) and its capital. There has been a city here for thousands of years, and in the old city you can still see traditional houses built around crumbling courtyards. But mind you don't lose your way in the twisting alleyways. Sadly, many old-style buildings have been replaced by modern ones. Luckily, some old customs never change so why not drop into a teahouse if you fancy a nice, refreshing cuppa?

Don't miss: The Forbidden City. This huge, walled city stands in the ancient city centre. It has hundreds of palaces, temples and other buildings. Only the emperor's family and advisors were allowed inside.

EPILOGUE

So that's it, folks, and sad to say, we've reached the end of the road. I don't think we've left anyone behind, unless someone's wandered off without their map. I hope you've enjoyed our wicked world tour and that I'll see you again soon. If you're like me, you won't be home for long before you'll be bitten by the travelling bug again. But for now, it's time to hang your battered boots up, put your souvenirs on a shelf, and bore your friends silly with your horrible holiday snaps.

But just before I say goodbye, I want to leave you with some wicked advice about travelling. Intrepid British explorer, Joseph Thomson (1858–1895) once said…

"He who goes slowly, goes safely.
He who goes safely, goes far."

By the way, his favourite trick for making friends with the locals he met was to keep taking out his two false front teeth and pretending it was magic. And amazingly, it worked a treat. Wherever you're heading next, be sure to take trick-playing Thomson's advice. Then you'll have the world at your itchy feet. Now there's a horrible thought. Goodbye!